AILA Review

Integrating Content and Language in Higher Education

VOLUME 25   2012

John Benjamins Publishing Company
Amsterdam/Philadelphia

Table of contents

Integrating content and language in higher education: An introduction
to English-medium policies, conceptual issues and research practices
across Europe   1
   Ute Smit and Emma Dafouz

Articles

ICL at the micro level: L2 speakers taking on the role of language experts   13
   Niina Hynninen

Focus on form in ICLHE lectures in Italy: Evidence from English-
medium science lectures by native speakers of Italian   30
   Francesca Costa

Academics' beliefs about language use and proficiency in Spanish
multilingual higher education   48
   Inmaculada Fortanet-Gómez

"I don't teach language." The linguistic attitudes of physics lecturers in
Sweden   64
   John Airey

English-medium programmes at Austrian business faculties: A status
quo survey on national trends and a case study on programme design
and delivery   80
   Barbara Unterberger

A postscript on institutional motivations, research concerns and
professional implications   101
   Christiane Dalton-Puffer

Integrating content and language in higher education

An introduction to English-medium policies, conceptual issues and research practices across Europe

Ute Smit and Emma Dafouz

Introducing the topic

The research developments of the last 15 years are a good indicator that Content and Language Integrated Learning (CLIL) has established itself as a widely used research framework for applied linguistic interests into educational undertakings that use a foreign or additional language for the teaching of curricular content. While content areas, such as geography, accounting, agriculture or aerodynamics, are highly diverse, the common denominator of CLIL scenarios is that the respective learners are engaged in a joint learning practice of subject matter and foreign language (e.g. Coyle, Hood and Marsh 2010; Dalton-Puffer 2011; Marsh & Wolff 2007). In view of the growing realities of such teaching and learning settings that distinguish themselves from foreign language educational practices (where the main focus is reaching proficiency in the target language), CLIL has shown wide applicability across regional and national contexts as well as all educational levels (e.g. Dafouz & Guerrini 2009; Dalton-Puffer, Nikula & Smit 2010; Ruiz de Zarobe, Sierra & Gallardo del Puerto 2011).

Initiated in Europe and stimulated by the European Union's general policy to enhance individual and societal multilingualism (e.g. European Commission 2012), CLIL, or mainstream education in a foreign or additional language, has rapidly gained in popularity in many countries with a tradition of exclusively using the dominant or national language(s) for educational purposes. Whether this recent trend towards enlarging the circle of medium languages will finally result in a paradigm shift away from what Gogolin (1994) fittingly called the 'monolingual habitus' of formal education towards a bi/multilingual one is too early to say, not least because the language chosen for instruction is first and foremost English. In any case, CLIL education raises questions about immutable principles and established practices in formal education.

Given the novelty and urgency of these educational changes, a vibrant research scene has established itself, for which CLIL seems to function well as an umbrella term for a myriad of bi/multilingual educational settings that nevertheless partially reflect different contextual parameters and are approached from diverse research interests (Dalton-Puffer 2007; Llinares, Morton & Whittaker 2012; Ruiz de Zarobe, Sierra & Gallardo del Puerto 2011; Smit 2010a). While the resulting conceptual openness might be in need of clarification, it reflects the dynamic developments of this recent phenomenon and, furthermore, provides researchers with a common point of reference in analysing their specific educational scenarios.

AILA Review 25 (2012), 1–12. DOI 10.1075/aila.25.01smi
ISSN 1461–0213 / E-ISSN 1570–5595 © John Benjamins Publishing Company

Founded in 2006 as a forum for exchange across local CLIL settings, the AILA Research Network (ReN) on "CLIL and Immersion Education: Applied Linguistic Perspectives" has been influential in making visible and interconnecting the many local research interests and undertakings in teaching and learning through an additional language that have been pursued all over Europe and increasingly over other parts of the world. The numerous ReN publications (Dalton-Puffer & Nikula 2006; Dalton-Puffer & Smit 2007; Dalton-Puffer, Nikula & Smit 2010a; Smit & Dalton-Puffer 2007; Smit, Schiftner & Dalton-Puffer 2010) are concerned with a wide range of linguistic and pedagogical research domains, such as target language proficiency, teacher and student motivation, teaching materials, language use in the classroom or curricular developments in CLIL contexts. As regards learner groups, however, these publications reveal a clear preponderance of primary and secondary education.

Against this backdrop, it is the aim of this *AILA Review* volume to complement the established CLIL research interest in compulsory education by focusing specifically on tertiary educational settings, since, as argued in detail below, university-level education constitutes a distinct research and educational field owing to its specific characteristics as regards language and education policy, institutional interests as well as learners and instructors involved (cf. Smit 2011).

Characterising education on the tertiary level

Concerning educational and language policies, the fundamental socio-political changes in tertiary education across Europe of the last two decades, generally identified as the "Bologna process" (Benelux Bologna Secretariat 2007–2010; European Ministers of Education 1999; Räisänen & Fortanet-Gómez 2008; Wilkinson 2008), have not only led to re-structuring university programmes and curricula, but have also made English-medium education a reality. Irrespective of region or educational tradition, European tertiary educational institutions have undergone a remarkable shift away from relying exclusively on their respective national or dominant language(s) towards widening the spectrum by also using English for teaching and learning. This has resulted in the need for new language measures, such as offering language support courses in the dominant educational language to incoming students, on the one hand, and, on the other, in English for specific and academic purposes. Given the complex interplay of global, (trans)national, regional and local needs and demands, these sociolinguistic developments display a strongly 'glocal' (Robertson 1995) character in that they are realised in a myriad of ways of using English as global language for local educational needs and aims.

English-medium university teaching or English-medium instruction (hereinafter EMI) outside Europe and its implications for speakers of other languages have already been a matter of academic concern for many decades, but, understandably, rather in areas with a long-standing tradition in using English as the main or only academic language (e.g. Banda 2009; Ferguson 2006; Lin & Martin 2005; Tsui & Tollefson 2007) in what Kachru's (e.g. 1992) still widely used model is referred to as the 'Inner' and 'Outer Circles'. Most European countries, however, do not fall into these circles and, moreover, have well-established higher educational systems in their respective national languages. The recently burgeoning use of English for communicational needs within and across universities is hence a new situation in need of focused attention. To put this unparalleled development into numbers: English-medium university courses all over continental Europe have tripled in the last decade, with around 2,400 English-medium programmes running mainly, but not only, in Germany, the Netherlands and Scandinavia (Wächter & Maiworm 2008). This figure represents an over 300 percent increase on the BA and MA programmes offered in 2002 (Doiz, Lasagabaster & Sierra 2011), which reveals that the European higher educational scene has been a highly fertile breeding ground for introducing English as a new medium of instruction and must thus be regarded as an ideal site for investigating the realities and implications of teaching and learning in an additional language.

As regards tertiary institutional interests, these recent policy developments go hand-in-hand with the general trend for universities to promote cross-border student mobility and international partnerships within the European Higher Education Area or EHEA (Knight 2008). In other words, internationalisation must be taken as one of the main reasons for using English as a medium of instruction across universities in Europe, with language learning remaining of secondary importance (cf. our final section below and also the contributions to this volume). English-medium teaching has thus become that popular because of the societal status and multiple roles of English — the 'global language' (Crystal 2003) also of international research and academic publications. Thanks to its additional status as the most widely learned second or foreign language (Graddol 2006: 62), English also often functions as the language bi/multilingual academics use for communication, i.e. as their lingua franca (Seidlhofer 2011). Research into English as a lingua franca (ELF) has foregrounded the general levels of success with which students as well as lecturers draw on English in order to meet their communicational ends, but also that such levels of success are only possible because of the interactants' willingness to invest time and energy in collaboratively co-constructing their exchanges across diverse multilingual repertoires (Björkman 2009; Mauranen & Ranta 2008; Smit 2010a). Additionally, the rich and continuously growing research literature into English used for specific purposes provides us with detailed descriptions of content-area specific genres that novices need to acquire in the process of developing their expertise (e.g. Bhatia 2004; Swales 2004). English used as a lingua franca within tertiary education can thus be expected to combine in interesting ways the shared linguistic repertoire available to the group of interlocutors in multilingual educational settings with their expertise in the respective content area and its genre-specific conventions (e.g. Smit 2010b; see also Hynninen and Airey, this volume).

Finally, and in addition to policy issues and institutional interests, university-level education is also specific with regards to the learners and instructors involved. In contrast to compulsory education, students at university have reached advanced levels of cognitive development and decided to further their education of their own accord. Furthermore, they have proven themselves successful learners and have accumulated a considerable amount of learning experience and expertise. Additionally, university-level students are expected to have a high level of English language proficiency and, given the increase in international mobility, tend to find themselves in linguistically and culturally heterogeneous groups. While English as a global language is clearly relevant to education at all stages, its dominant position as main language of academia and transnational research across disciplines adds a type of communicative need within higher education that is unparalleled in primary and secondary educational contexts. Research and its relevance for a university career is also a key factor in distinguishing tertiary teaching staff from their colleagues at the compulsory level. Thus, while the latter are primarily identified as teachers, and generally receive pedagogical education in preparation for that profession, the former are largely defined according to their role as researchers, which is also reflected in the fact that tertiary teaching staff seldom obtain any substantial pedagogical training. Finally, tertiary institutions tend to be relatively autonomous in their curricular planning decisions.

Terminological considerations
Having established why this volume focuses on English-medium instruction at European universities, what still remains to be discussed is the conundrum of which notion to use in order to address the research topic of the present *AILA Review* volume. Presently, the pertinent literature works with terms such as English-medium teaching (Coleman 2006), English-medium instruction or EMI (Hellekjaer 2010), CLIL (e.g. Dalton-Puffer, Smit & Nikula 2010b) and Integrating Content and Language in Higher Education or ICLHE (Wilkinson & Zegers 2007), a label, which was originally

coined for the first conference on the theme held in Maastricht in 2004 (cf. also Wilkinson 2004). While some recent studies seem to utilise all of these terms interchangeably (e.g. Doiz, Lasagabaster & Sierra 2011), others make referential distinctions which can be traced to different conceptualisations of the term.

Most prominently, some of the CLIL literature offers a more focalized, pedagogically inspired model defined as "a dual-focused educational approach" which aims explicitly at a "fusion" of both subject content and language learning (Coyle, Hood & Marsh 2010: 41–45). Consequently, practices lacking such fused pedagogical teaching aims would not fall into prototypical CLIL programmes. The same pedagogical considerations have been used when focusing exclusively on the tertiary level, which has led to 'ICLHE' being reserved for those programmes that have "explicit and integrated content and language learning aims" (Unterberger & Wilhelmer 2011: 95), in contrast to 'EMI', which focuses on content learning only (ibid.). While this distinction clarifies the pedagogical model adopted, the notion of "content and language integration" can also be interpreted with regard to discursive classroom practices, whereby the interactants co-construct meaning and their topics. From such a discursive perspective, integrating content and language (ICL) is understood as an integral part of the teaching and learning practices and can thus be seen as taking place irrespective of explicit teaching aims. From such a point of view, then, EMI would foreground the research focus on instruction, while ICL would concentrate on the ongoing teacher–student discourse as integral part of teaching and learning (cf. Smit 2010a: 33).

In other words, the defining criteria for EMI and ICL depend strongly on the general research focus adopted. In an attempt to acknowledge and come to terms with the resulting terminological dilemma, we have decided to use both in the title of this publication in a complementary manner. While we fully support the socio-cultural view of learning and its fundamentally discursive nature, we also recognise that it is the choice of medium of instruction that necessitates such research in the first place. In view of the complexity of the matter and the fact that the individual contributions to this volume pursue different research foci, we are suggesting a combined view, and will use EMI/ICL in the rest of the introduction, while each of the individual contributions employs and introduces the terminology fitting to its specific conceptual take.

Overview of the volume

Classroom discourse

As indicated above, one central concern in EMI/ICL is the nature of classroom discourse, which we understand as comprising all meaning-constructing practices within an educational setting, be they spoken, written or computer-mediated. Clearly, such classroom practices are intricately contingent on the social players involved in their respective educational setting, thus being highly contextualised and constituting what van Lier (2004) identifies as micro-systems within the EMI/ICL approach. This means that classroom discourse comes with a high degree of situatedness (Lave & Wenger 1991), therefore resulting in cross-situational diversity. At the same time, this classroom discourse angle permits direct, unfiltered access to what is going on in the classroom, irrespective of what programme organisers and lecturers envisage for their specific course, and also irrespective of what role, if any, language learning might play for them. In other words, this approach to classroom discourse captures EMI/ICL 'at the grassroots' and, by covering actual classroom practices, allows researchers to develop their descriptions and interpretations of the teaching and learning processes in a bottom-up rather than a top-down manner. Research questions are manifold and far from having been analysed sufficiently, but to date several studies have collected relevant data in order to investigate, for instance, lecturing practices (Dafouz-Milne & Núñez-Perucha 2010; Dafouz, Núñez

& Sancho 2007; Morell 2004), student constructions of disciplinary content (Airey 2009, 2010), or the long-term discursive developments in English as the only shared language of a specific educational community (e.g. Smit 2010a). In addition to their detailed results on discursive patterns, generic specificities and dynamic speaker roles, such studies also offer insights into what 'content and language integration' at the tertiary level can look like and the pedagogical implications it might have (e.g. Fortanet-Gomez & Räisänen 2008; Gustafsson 2011; Wilkinson 2004; Wilkinson & Zegers 2007).

This volume includes two such studies (Costa and Hynninen), both drawing on corpora of English-medium classroom talk in technical, agricultural and natural scientific subjects. While both studies focus their analyses on metalingual comments, i.e. sequences that topicalise language rather than preceding discourse and its interpretation (cf. Hynninen, this volume, referring to Berry 2005), they complement each other in view of their different although complementary research interests. Francesca Costa's investigation concentrates on lecturer talk in selected lectures given at three Italian universities to predominantly Italian and some international students. Embedded in the Focus on Form (FonF) framework of second/foreign language learning (Long & Robinson 1998; Lyster 2007), Costa analyses lecturers' metalingual comments and, in line with the bilingual nature of the discourse, extends the FonF framework by integrating code-switching as additional strategy in foregrounding formal aspects. Niina Hynninen's study is set at Helsinki University, where she investigates classroom-based discussions within international groups of students and mainly content-expert teachers. As befitting to the multilinguality of these groups, this study is framed in an 'English as a lingua franca' (ELF) paradigm (e.g. Mauranen & Ranta 2009; Seidlhofer 2011) and is concerned with how the native and non-native speaker students and teachers construct and negotiate the role of language "expert".

In brief, these two contributions illustrate the value of metalingual comments as point of access to how language-focused classroom talk in EMI classes makes ICL possible, while, at the same time, they underline how each of the two research interests pursued offers relevant insights into (incidental) language teaching and learning. In view of their complementarity, their findings point towards the need to develop a combined approach that integrates the focus of ELF on language use and of FonF on language learning.

Teacher cognition
Given the aforementioned minimal concern with pedagogical matters in higher education in the relevant EMI/ICL literature, it is not surprising that attention to university teachers' beliefs, opinions and attitudes about education and teaching practices in general has been rather scarce. Following conceptualizations of teaching as a process of active decision-making informed by teachers' thoughts (Borg 2011; Cowie 2011; Feryok 2010) the term 'teacher cognition' has come to encompass a multiplicity of labels that, by and large, include "the beliefs, knowledge, theories, assumptions and attitudes about all aspects of their work which teachers have" (Borg 1999: 22). The primary implication of this approach is that an understanding of the often implicit psychological bases of teachers' work is necessary if indeed we are to move beyond a superficial behavioural conception of instructional processes. Although studies on teacher cognition come mostly from mainstream education or EFL settings (see Woods 1996; Borg 1999, 2003 for a comprehensive review in the language teaching context), some recent work has focused specifically on teachers' reflections in CLIL contexts (Huettner, Dalton-Puffer & Smit, forthcoming; Moate 2011; Morton 2012).

This publication contains two studies that draw on university teachers' opinions and attitudes towards EMI/ICL courses, but without using the teacher cognition label. The first, by Inmaculada Fortanet, uses a questionnaire to tap into academics' self-assessed competence of the three different

languages used at the Universitat Jaume I (Spanish, English and Valencian), as well as their different roles within academia. Her analysis reveals differences in the teaching practices implemented,
depending both on the academics' subject discipline and professional profile (content or language
experts), a preference towards English and Spanish as instructional languages at postgraduate level
in detriment of the local language (Valencian) for the sake of internationalisation, and, finally, a
lack of pedagogical awareness mainly among the content teachers surveyed. The second article, by
John Airey, uses a phenomenographic approach to analyse the opinions of physics lecturers from
four Swedish universities. Following the notion of disciplinary knowledge construction (Bernstein
1999), the author places physics within a hierarchical disciplinary model and explains, against this
framework, the coincidental views, opinions and teaching practices exhibited by the physics teachers interviewed.

In sum, these two papers, although methodologically different, share a common interest in
teacher cognition and its impact on their daily practice, and reflect the irrefutable need to take
stakeholders' underlying beliefs into account when aiming at successful educational innovations (cf.
also Markee 2001).

English-medium policy
Given the growing "marketization" of tertiary education and the autonomy of each institution, language policy considerations are a major concern. More precisely, what is of interest is not only which
decisions are taken as regards language use in and around under- and postgraduate programmes,
but also why these are taken and in which ways they are carried through in actual educational
practices. In other words, language policy is concerned with "language choices made by individual
speakers on the basis of rule-governed patterns recognized by the speech community (or communities) of which they are members" (Spolsky 2009: 1) and is thus interested in more than simply
policy documents. Clearly, these are relevant for the 'rule-governed patterns', but so are beliefs held
about which language should be used when, for what purpose and by whom. And both, managerial
documents and widely shared beliefs are intricately interrelated with actual language practices. The
resulting "expanded view of [language policy]" (Shohamy 2006: 32) also recognises that the three
components — language management, language beliefs, language practices (Spolsky 2004) — do
not fit neatly together, but, on the contrary, they tend to stand in competition, reflecting the diverse
interests and language ideologies of different societal groups (Shohamy 2006: 45).

With such a comprehensive and dynamic understanding of language policy in mind, an investigation of the language choices discussed, laid down and lived out at a specific university will need
to foreground the local specificities and, at the same time, cast its investigative net wide enough to
capture more than simply policy statements (cf. e.g. Doiz, Lasagabaster & Sierra 2012; Räisänen &
Fortanet-Gomez 2008; Wilkinson 2004). One of the papers included in this volume (Unterberger) is
a case in point as it provides an overview of business education at Austrian universities. The national
research frame that Barbara Unterberger applies allows the reader to gain comparative insights into
the relevance of English for business studies across institutions in a traditionally German-speaking
country. At the same time, the paper focuses in particular on the Vienna University of Economics
and Business, the only Austrian university exclusively dedicated to business studies, and offers a
detailed discussion of the various English-medium programmes by drawing on policy statements as
well as interview data with the programme directors. In other words, the paper takes a multilayered
view of language policy by combining managerial statements with stakeholder assessment and beliefs, thus revealing the complexity of EMI/ICL practices. Additionally, it identifies the complex and
dynamic interplay of various factors, such as the need for internationalisation of students and staff,
and the pull of English as an academic language: as a lingua franca in multilingual groups. At the

same time, the analysis also discusses the limits imposed by the use of English, such as those derived from by the imponderabilities of setting up cross-disciplinary collaboration between content and language experts, and the concomitant need to take a more holistic, multilingual view on language policy.

EMI/ICL research — a critical view

As argued for so far, EMI/ICL in European higher education is not only developing into a widely spread educational practice, but also requires concerted research undertakings from various points of view. This volume focuses on three such perspectives, viz. classroom discourse as the site of teaching and learning practices in the making, teacher cognition that foregrounds teachers as central agents in implementing educational approaches, and English-medium policy documents and implementation as the dynamic framework within which EMI/ICL realities are developing.

While we do not claim that these three foci suffice in discussing EMI/ICL, they allow for in-depth analyses and findings whose relevance goes well beyond the individual case under the spotlight. As the only directly accessible 'point of access' to the teaching and learning process, research into classroom discourse in EMI/ICL settings offers insights into how adults make use of English as their additional language in constructing and becoming familiar with topics and expert concerns in their diverse areas of specialisation. Additionally, such findings are invaluable for higher education pedagogy and provide information on the kind of pedagogical education and training university lecturers would profit from when using English as medium of instruction. The same is true for studies focussing on the views and beliefs lecturers have regarding EMI/ICL. In addition to establishing what those carrying out the educational innovations actually think about them, such investigations add relevant information to developing tailor-made and success-prone in-service education and training courses. Finally, there are many tertiary educational institutions that have enlarged their traditional programmes by English-medium courses. They still need to be analysed as regards their expanded policy approach, aiming for a critical and informed assessment of the respective practices, beliefs and relevant documents. Once a broader base of such analyses is available, research could go beyond the description of individual cases and embark on a more generally applicable model of constructing and implementing English-medium policy in tertiary institutions.

In addition to its relevance to research into higher education, the still young, but fast developing EMI/ICL research scene has potential for educational concerns further afield, especially so because English in its various roles has become an important factor in education more generally. In this day and age, more and more learner groups and their teachers, also at secondary and even primary level need to use English, either because of it being the only lingua franca shared by the participants in a given setting or because of the use of teaching materials that come in English. Furthermore and going beyond school-based education, the growing relevance of English used for diverse occupational purposes is also increasingly central in the corporate world, resulting in a myriad of in-company English language trainings, which aim to help staff stay up-to-date in their fields.

Although the three perspectives covered in this volume complement each other by dealing with the actual discursive practices, stakeholders' perceptions as well as institutional decisions, we do not wish to claim that they cover EMI/ICL realities in their entirety. Rather, there are further concerns that need focussed attention, three of which we will sketch in the following.

First of all, the geographical scope adopted in this volume needs to be complemented with discussions of EMI/ICL realities beyond the national borders here covered, both within Europe (i.e. Eastern countries) and also across the world. In Japan, for example, Brady (2008: 97) reports that both governmental and private educational authorities have urged universities to offer a percentage (10–30%) of their academic courses in English and that a number of institutions have indeed followed these recommendations, although they continue to teach English mainly as a language subject rather than integrated within content. Shifting continents, the studies by Jacobs (2007) and Wright (2007) in South Africa portray a different context where the integration of language issues and disciplinary focus is revisited from the point of view of language specialists and content specialists in an attempt to join efforts (cf. also Gustafsson 2011). Moreover, it is our belief that more instances of true multilingualism in higher education, although still minoritarian, might gain strength in the coming years as university internationalisation becomes a consolidated reality. Initial studies in trilingual settings (e.g. Fortanet, this volume; Doiz, Lasagabaster & Sierra 2011, 2012; Veronesi & Nickenig 2009) already point at some of the challenges, but also the merits of fostering more than two languages in an attempt to serve the local as well as international needs of universities in the 21st century. Further research describing and comparing contexts and languages of instruction would be most welcome in an attempt to grasp further insights into the realities outside our immediate European Union context.

Furthermore, an appeal for more interdisciplinary collaboration amongst the stakeholders involved in EMI/ICL settings is also lodged here. To date, as most of the published research confirms, the driving force to integrate language and content in higher education is clearly one-sided and comes mainly from linguists, language teachers and teacher educators. In contrast, politicians, university authorities, administrators, as well as part of the lecturing staff (i.e. content specialists) have initially engaged in this new scenario by embracing a top-down internationalisation plan alongside a chance for professional and academic development; a scenario wherein pedagogical concerns and, more specifically, language learning matters are usually of secondary importance. In our view, nevertheless, it is of vital significance to bridge the gap between the parties involved so that this educational practice can reach its full potential. One way of attracting all stakeholders' interest in the implications of EMI/ICL in tertiary education is by investigating student learning outcomes, both content and language-focused. After all, it is by undertaking studies on learners' academic and linguistic achievement that the validity of this approach can be assessed. While the research literature is still remarkably thin on truly interdisciplinary studies, the first collaborative research steps of the Faculty of Economics and Business Administration and the Department of English Language and Linguistics at the Complutense University (Madrid) show that disciplinary and language experts can work together and jointly deliver more comprehensive findings than each expert could do individually (Camacho, Dafouz & Urquía, submitted). Overall, then, there is an urgent need to provide information on, and raise awareness of the educational and linguistic implications entailed in the internationalisation process that the university is undergoing worldwide.

Finally, the underlying forces of contextualisation, on the one hand, and harmonization, on the other, have important but potentially contradictory implications for EMI/ICL in higher education. While the European slogan of "unity in diversity" tries to offer a conciliatory view on how these forces could interact, their centrifugal nature should neither be overlooked nor downplayed. As implied in the previous discussions of language policies, supranational, national and local strategies can, and often are, in conflict with each other. Equally, pedagogical considerations that come into play can contradict each other, especially if there is a mismatch between teacher cognition and the educational changes implemented, as entrenched power hierarchies across institutions are difficult to modify. Moreover, prevailing epistemological and cultural differences across disciplines (Donald 2009; Lueddeke 2003; Neumann 2001) may also reveal profound divergences across contexts which are well-worth researching. Studies into EMI/ICL contexts should also take into account that, as a result of internationalisation, curricular harmonization across Europe could eventually lead to content harmonization and, ultimately, to a gradual loss of diversity across university teaching from a linguistic, methodological or disciplinary perspective. Language-related concerns have already been voiced in as much as the predominant use of English for academic purposes is seen as, on the one hand, threatening the functional breadth of previously fully established languages such as, for example, Swedish (see Airey, this volume; Shaw et al. 2008), and, on the other hand, as precluding academic discourse and, more importantly, its ideas from the generally interested public not proficient enough in English (Ammon & McConnell 2002; Carli & Ammon 2007; Ehlich 2000). As it is to be expected that the effects of harmonization will not stop at the language-level, we consider it high time to start investigating what consequences this process is having on the teaching and constructing of disciplinary knowledge across linguistically and culturally heterogeneous educational settings.

The preceding account of the three, so far under-researched research foci (i.e. EMI/ICL beyond well researched areas, interdisciplinary collaboration of content and language specialists, the wider socio-political and pedagogical effects of EMI/ICL policies) cannot do more than sketch extant research gaps in EMI/ICL. Nonetheless, we hope that these thoughts, together with the contributions to this volume of *AILA Review*, will inspire readers to develop and participate in new research projects that delve into English-medium higher education in areas with a tradition of L1 tertiary institutions, by ideally combining various of the (applied) linguistic, subject disciplinary and pedagogical, as well as higher educational research interests at stake.

References

Airey, J. 2009. Estimating undergraduate bilingual scientific literacy in Sweden. *International CLIL Research Journal* 1(2): 26–35.

Airey, J. 2010. The ability of students to explain science concepts in two languages. *Hermes — Journal of Language and Communication Studies* 45: 35–49.

Ammon, U. & McConnell, G. 2002. *English as an Academic Language in Europe. A Survey of its Use in Teaching*. Frankfurt: Peter Lang.

Banda, F. 2009. Critical perspectives on language planning and policy in Africa: Accounting for the notion of multilingualism. *SPIL (Stellenbosch Papers in Linguistics) PLUS. Special Issue: Multilingualism and Language Policies in Africa* 38: 1–11.

Benelux Bologna Secretariat. 2007–2010. The official Bologna process website, July 2007–June 2010, ⟨http://www.ond.vlaanderen.be/hogeronderwijs/bologna/⟩ (15 May 2012).

Bernstein, M. 1999. Vertical and horizontal discourse: An essay. *British Journal of Sociology Education* 20: 157–173.

Berry, R. 2005. Making the most of metalanguage. *Language Awareness* 14(1): 3–20.

Bhatia, V.K. 2004. *Worlds of Written Discourse. A Genre-based View*. London: Continuum.

Björkman, B. 2009. From Code to Discourse in Spoken ELF. In *English as a Lingua Franca: Studies and Findings*, A. Mauranen & E. Ranta (eds), 225–251. Newcastle upon Tyne: Cambridge Scholars Publishing.

Borg, S. 1999. Studying teacher cognition in second language grammar teaching. *System* 27: 19–31.

Borg, S. 2003. Teacher cognition in language teaching: A review of research on what teachers think, know, believe and do. *Language Teaching* 36: 81–109.

Borg, S. 2011. The impact of in-service teacher education on language teachers' beliefs. *System*, 39(3): 370–380.

Brady, A. 2008. Developing a civic education vision and practice for foreign-additional-other (FAO) language and content integration in higher education. In *Realizing Content and Language Integration in Higher Education*, R. Wilkinson & V. Zegers (eds), 96–109. Maastricht: Maastricht University Language Centre.

Carli, A. & Ammon, U. (eds). 2007. *AILA Review 20: Linguistic Inequality in Scientific Communication Today*. Amsterdam: John Benjamins.

Cowie, N. 2011. Emotions that experienced English as a foreign language (EFL) teachers feel about their students, their colleagues and their work. *Teaching and Teacher Education* 27(1): 235–242.

Camacho, M.; Dafouz, E. & Urquía, E. submitted. "Surely they can't do as well": Business students' learning strategies and academic outcomes in English-Medium Instruction.

Coleman, J. 2006. English-medium teaching in European higher education. *Language Teaching* 39(1): 1–14.

Coyle, D.; Hood, P. & Marsh, D. 2010. *CLIL. Content and Language Integrated Learning*. Cambridge: Cambridge University Press.

Crystal, D. 2003. *English as a Global Language*. (2nd ed.). Cambridge: Cambridge University Press.

Dafouz, E. & Guerrini, M.C. (eds). 2009. *CLIL across Educational Levels*. Madrid: Richmond.

Dafouz, E., Núñez, B. & Sancho, C. 2007. Analysing stance in a CLIL university context: non-native speaker use of personal pronouns and modal verbs. *International Journal of Bilingualism and Bilingual Education* 10(5): 647–662.

Dafouz-Milne, E. & Núñez-Perucha, B. 2010. Metadiscursive devices in university lectures: a contrastive analysis of L1 and L2 teacher performance. In *Language Use and Language Learning in CLIL Classrooms*, Dalton-Puffer, C.; Nikula, T. & Smit, U. (eds), 213–232. Amsterdam: John Benjamins.

Dalton-Puffer, C. 2007. *Discourse in Content and Language Integrated Learning (CLIL) Classrooms*. Amsterdam: John Benjamins.

Dalton-Puffer, C. 2011. Content and language integrated learning: from practice to principles? *Annual Review of Applied Linguistics* 31: 182–204.

Dalton-Puffer, C. & Nikula, T. (eds). 2006. *Current Research on CLIL. VIEWS — Vienna English Working Papers* [Special issue] 15(3).

Dalton-Puffer, C., Nikula, T. & Smit, U. (eds). 2010a. *Language Use and Language Learning in CLIL Classroom*. Amsterdam: John Benjamins.

Dalton-Puffer, C., Nikula, T. & Smit, U. 2010b. Language use and language learning in CLIL: Current findings and contentious issues. In *Language Use and Language Learning in CLIL Classrooms*, Dalton-Puffer, C., Nikula, T. & Smit, U. (eds), 279–291. Amsterdam: John Benjamins.

Dalton-Puffer, C. & Smit, U. (eds). 2007. *Empirical Perspectives on CLIL Classroom Discourse*. Frankfurt: Peter Lang.

Doiz, A., Lasagabaster, D. & Sierra, J. 2011. Internationalisation, multilingualism and English-medium instruction. *World Englishes* 30 (3): 345–359.

Doiz, A., Lasagabaster, D. & Sierra, J. 2012. Globalisation, internationalisation, multilingualism and linguistic strains in higher education. *Studies in Higher Education*: 1–15.

Donald, J.G. 2009. The commons: Disciplinary and interdisciplinary encounters. In *The University and its Disciplines: Teaching and Learning Within and Beyond Disciplinary Boundaries*, C. Kreber (ed), 36–49. New York: Routledge.

Ehlich, K. 2000. Deutsch als Wissenschaftssprache für das 21. Jahrhundert. *German as a Foreign Language* 1: 47–63.

European Commission. 2012. Languages 2010 and beyond. ⟨http://ec.europa.eu/languages/languages-of-europe/languages-2010-and-beyond_en.htm⟩ (19 September 2012)

European Ministers of Education. 1999. The Bologna declaration of 19 June 1999: Joint declaration of the European ministers of education, ⟨http://www.ond.vlaanderen.be/hogeronderwijs/bologna/documents/MDC/BOLOGNA_DECLARATION1.pdf⟩ (19 September 2012).

Feryok, A. 2010. Language teacher cognitions: Complex dynamic systems? *System* 38(2): 272–279.

Ferguson, G. 2006. *Language Planning and Education*. Edinburgh: Edinburgh University Press.

Fortanet-Gómez, I. & Räisänen, C. (eds). 2008. *ESP in European Higher Education. Integrating Language and Content*. Amsterdam: John Benjamins.

Gogolin, I. 1994. *Der monolinguale Habitus der multilingualen Schule*. Münster: Waxmann.

Graddol, D. 2006. *English Next. Why Global English May Mean the End of 'English as a Foreign Language'*. British Council.

Gustafsson, M. (ed). 2011. *Collaborating for Content and Language Integrated Learning* [Special Issue]. *Across the Disciplines* 8(3), ⟨http://wac.colostate.edu/atd/clil/index.cfm⟩ (19 September 2012).

Hellekjaer, G. 2010. Language matters: Assessing lecture comprehension in Norwegian English-medium higher education. In *Language Use and Language Learning in CLIL Classrooms*, C. Dalton-Puffer, T. Nikula & U. Smit (eds), 233–258. Amsterdam: John Benjamins.

Hüttner, J., Dalton-Puffer, C. & Smit, U. forthcoming. The power of beliefs: Lay theories and their influence on the implementation of CLIL programmes. *International Journal of Bilingualism and Bilingual Education*.

Jacobs, C. 2007. Integrating content and language: Whose job is it anyway? In *Researching Content and Language Integration in Higher Education*, R. Wilkinson & V. Zegers (eds), 35–47. Nijmegen: Valkhof Pers.

Kachru, B.B. (ed). 1992. The *Other Tongue. English Across Cultures*. (2nd ed). Urbana: University of Illinois Press.

Knight, J. 2008. *Higher Education in Turmoil: The Changing World of Internationalisation*. Rotterdam: Sense Publishers.

Lave, L. & Wenger, E. 1991. *Situated Learning: Legitimate Peripheral Participation*. Cambridge: Cambridge University Press.

Lin, A.M.Y & Martin, P.W. (eds). 2005. *Decolonisation, Globalisation. Language-in-Education Policy and Practice*. Bristol: Multilingual Matters.

Llinares, A., Morton, T. & Whittaker. R. 2012. *The Roles of Language in CLIL*. Cambridge: Cambridge University Press.

Long, M.H. & Robinson, P. 1998. Focus on form. Theory, research and practice. In *Focus on Form in Classroom Second Language Acquisition*, C. Doughty & J. Williams (eds), 15–41. Cambridge: Cambridge University Press.

Lueddeke, G.R. 2003. Professionalising teaching practice in higher education: A study of disciplinary variation and 'teaching scholarship'. *Studies in Higher Education* 28(2): 213–228.

Lyster, R. 2007. *Learning and Teaching Languages through Content*. Amsterdam: John Benjamins.

Markee, N. 2001. The diffusion of innovation. In *Innovation in English Language Teaching*, D. Hall & A. Hewings (eds), 118–126. London: Routledge.

Marsh, D. & Wolff, D. (eds). 2007. *Diverse Contexts — Converging Goals. CLIL in Europe*. Frankfurt: Peter Lang.

Mauranen, A. & Ranta, E. 2008. English as an academic lingua franca — the ELFA project. *Nordic Journal of English Studies* 7(3): 199–202.

Mauranen, A. & Ranta, E. (eds). 2009. *English as a Lingua Franca. Studies and Findings*. Cambridge: Cambridge Scholars Publishing.

Moate, J. 2011. The impact of foreign language mediated teaching on the sense of teachers' professional integrity in the classroom. *European Journal of Teacher Education* 34(3): 333–346.

Morell, T. 2004. Interactive lecture discourse for university EFL students. *English for Specific Purposes* 23: 325–338.

Morton, T. 2012. Classroom talk, conceptual change and teacher reflection in bilingual science teaching. *Teaching and Teacher Education* 28: 101–110.

Neumann, R. 2001. Disciplinary differences in university teaching. *Studies in Higher Education* 26(2): 135–146.

Räisänen, C. & Fortanet-Gómez, I. 2008. The state of ESP teaching and learning in Western European higher education after Bologna. In *ESP in European Higher Education. Integrating Language and Content*, I. Fortanet-Gómez & C. Räisänen (eds), 11–51. Amsterdam: John Benjamins.

Robertson, R. 1995. Glocalization. Time-space and homogeneity-heterogeneity. In *Global Modernities*, M. Featherstone, S. Lash & R. Robertson (eds), 25–44. Thousand Oaks, CA: Sage.

Ruiz de Zarobe, Y., Sierra, J. M. & Gallardo del Puerto, F. (eds). 2011. *Content and Foreign Language Integrated Learning. Contributions to Multilingualism in European Contexts*. Bern: Peter Lang.

Seidlhofer, B. 2011. *Understanding English as a Lingua Franca*. Oxford: Oxford University Press.

Shaw, P., Benson, C., Brunsberg, S., Druhs, R. & Minugh, D. 2008. Preparing for international masters degrees at Stockholm University and the Royal Institute of Technology in Stockholm. In *ESP in European Higher*

Education. Integrating Language and Content, I. Fortanet-Gómez & C.A. Räisänen (eds), 267–282. Amsterdam: John Benjamins.

Shohamy, E. 2006. *Language Policy. Hidden Agendas and New Approaches*. London: Routledge.

Smit, U. & Dalton-Puffer, C. (eds). 2007. *Current Research on CLIL 2. VIEWS — Vienna English Working Papers* [Special issue] 16(3).

Smit, U. 2010a. *English as a Lingua Franca in Higher Education. A Longitudinal Study of Classroom Discourse*. Berlin: De Gruyter Mouton.

Smit, U. 2010b. Conceptualising English as a lingua franca (ELF) as a tertiary classroom language. *Stellenbosch Papers in Linguistics* 39: 59–74.

Smit, U. 2011. CLIL at the tertiary level. Contribution to the Research Network Symposium "CLIL and Immersion Education: Applied Linguistic Perspectives", 16th AILA World Congress in Beijing, China; 26 August.

Smit, U., Schiftner, B. & Dalton-Puffer, C. (eds). 2010. *Current Research on CLIL 3. VIEWS — Vienna English Working Papers* [Special issue] 19(3).

Spolsky, B. 2004. *Language Policy*. Cambridge: Cambridge University Press.

Spolsky, B. 2009. *Language Management*. Cambridge: Cambridge University Press.

Swales, J.M. 2004. *Research Genres. Explorations and Applications*. Cambridge: Cambridge University Press.

Tsui, A.B.M. & Tollefson, J.W. (eds). 2007. *Language Policy, Culture and Identity in Asian Contexts*. Mahwah, NJ: Lawrence Erlbaum.

Unterberger, B. & Wilhelmer, N. 2011. English-medium education in economics and business studies: capturing the status quo at Austrian universities. *International Journal of Applied Linguistics* 161: 90–110.

Van Lier, L. 2004. *The Ecology and Semiotics of Language Learning: A Sociocultural Perspective*. Boston: Kluwer Academic.

Veronesi, D. & Nickenig, D. (eds). 2009. *Bi- and Multilingual Universities: European Perspectives and Beyond. Conference Proceedings*. Bozen-Bolzano: Bozen-Bolzano University Press.

Wächter, B. & Maiworm, F. 2008. *English-Taught Programmes in European Higher Education: The Picture in 2007*. Bonn: Lemmens.

Wilkinson, R. (ed). 2004. *Integrating Content and Language. Meeting the Challenge of a Multilingual Higher Education; Proceedings of the ICL Conference, October 23–25 2003*. Maastricht: Universitaire Pers Maastricht.

Wilkinson, R. & Zegers, V. (eds). 2007. *Researching Content and Language Integration in Higher Education*. Nijmegen: Valkhof Pers.

Wilkinson, R. 2008. Locating the ESP space in problem-based learning: English-medium degree programmes from a post-Bologna perspective. In *ESP in European Higher Education: Integrating Language and Content*, I. Fortanet-Gómez & C. A. Räisänen, (eds), 55–73. Amsterdam: John Benjamins.

Woods, D. 1996. *Teacher Cognition in Language Teaching*. Cambridge: Cambridge University Press.

Wright, J. 2007. Key themes emerging from co-authoring during a content and language integration project. In *Researching Content and Language Integration in Higher Education*, R. Wilkinson & V. Zegers (eds), 82–95. Nijmegen: Valkhof Pers.

Authors' affiliations and e-mail addresses

Ute Smit
Universität Wien, Austria

ute.smit@univie.ac.at

Emma Dafouz
Universidad Complutense de Madrid, Spain

edafouz@filol.ucm.es

ICL at the micro level

L2 speakers taking on the role of language experts

Niina Hynninen

This paper focuses on the construction of language expertise in international, university-level English-medium courses where English is used as a lingua franca. Even if the courses are not language courses, language sometimes becomes the topic of discussion in the form of language correcting and commentary. This paper looks into these instances, where the teachers (i.e. subject experts) and students can be seen to take on, or be allotted, the role of language experts. The findings show that this role can be (1) based on a speaker's professional role and expertise in the relevant subject, (2) allotted to a native speaker of English, (3) negotiated between speakers, or (4) assigned to an English instructor. The paper discusses the implications of who takes on the role of language expert, and considers, in particular, to what extent the role still falls on native speakers of English. It will be shown that non-native speakers of English take on the role of language experts, and that this has implications for the kind of regulation done in the lingua franca interaction. The findings shed light on the micro-level realisation of Integrating Content and Language in Higher Education.

Introduction

As a result of the increase in English-medium instruction (EMI) in higher education institutions outside English-speaking countries (e.g. Graddol 2006: 73–80), more and more students and teachers (i.e. subject experts) communicate by using English as the shared language, a lingua franca. Despite this prominence of the lingua franca use of English, only some studies have focused on the interaction in English-medium courses from this perspective (e.g. Björkman 2008; Knapp 2011a, 2011b). Specifically, research on integrating content and language (ICL) in higher education and research on English as a lingua franca (ELF) are typically not brought together (for an exception, see Smit 2010). This paper, with its focus on the micro-level of EMI, is an attempt to bring the two research traditions closer together. In order to consider practices of integrating content and language at the micro-level of EMI, I explore which language expert roles the students and teachers construct as relevant when communicating in English-medium courses. The aim of this study, then, is to find out how language expertise is constructed in ELF interaction in EMI settings: who takes on the role of language expert, who is assigned that role, and what 'normative' authorities become relevant for the speakers. A further aim is to consider the implications of the expertise construction on the kind of regulation done in ELF interaction.

The data used in this study come from the University of Helsinki, Finland, a prime example of a higher education institution where the last decade has resulted in a surge of new English-medium

AILA Review 25 (2012), 13–29. DOI 10.1075/aila.25.02hyn
ISSN 1461–0213 / E-ISSN 1570–5595 © John Benjamins Publishing Company

degree programmes. The data consist of audio-recordings of ELF interaction in English-medium course and group-work meetings (see Method section). In the analysis, I focus on what language expert roles the students and teachers construct in the interaction. I approach language expertise in the interaction by considering: (a) who corrects and comments on their interlocutors' language, that is, who takes on the role of language expert, and (b) who is asked to correct or comment, that is, who is allotted the role of language expert. By focusing on these aspects of ELF interaction, it is possible to see what 'normative' authorities are constructed as relevant in the interaction, and what role ELF speakers take in the process (cf. Smit 2010). Since the data come from EMI in higher education, the findings are important in demonstrating ways in which content and language are integrated in the practice of EMI — and ways in which language questions are taken up even if language is not the topic of the course or group work.

The findings further shed light on the question of ownership of English from the perspective of ELF speakers. The spread of English has prompted scholars to discuss who can have custody over English, or the authority for codification of English. This has been done both in relation to World Englishes (e.g. Kachru 1996) and increasingly for the use of English in lingua franca settings (Jenkins 2000; Seidlhofer 2009, 2011). The discussions have led to a reconsideration of the role of native speakers of English in how English develops in the world, and the questioning of native speaker (NS) ownership of English (as argued, for instance, in Widdowson 1994), which in turn has raised the question of who 'should' propose standards for the use of ELF (Jenkins 2000). These conceptual considerations are important for adjusting paradigms for the teaching and testing of English to better respond to the use of English in today's world (see Canagarajah 2006). In this paper, however, I move from the conceptual level to the level of interaction in ELF to see to what extent speakers of ELF can be seen to question the so called NS ownership of English.

Before turning to the analysis, I describe the situation of EMI at the University of Helsinki, and introduce the ELF approach adopted in this study.

EMI at the University of Helsinki

At the University of Helsinki, along with a number of individual courses arranged in English, there are over 35 international, English-medium master's degree programmes, all of which have been established after the turn of the millennium (E. Koponen, international education adviser, personal communication, 25 January 2012). This reflects a general trend within the last decade, with an unprecedented spread of international degree programmes run in English in higher education institutions outside English-speaking countries (e.g. Graddol 2006: 73–80; Wächter 2008). Within Europe, higher education measures have been taken to harmonise degree structures across European countries, and to promote student and teacher mobility in an attempt to create a European Higher Education Area (Räisänen & Fortanet-Gómez 2008: 14–18; see Bologna Process). Especially the encouragement for mobility can be seen to increase the need for higher education institutions to establish courses and degree programmes run in an international language — most frequently English — to attract international students and staff. That English should be the international language chosen is probably due to its status as a global lingua franca, which increases the chances for *worldwide* student and staff mobility. Finland, along with other European countries with small national languages, is among the countries that most readily have embraced the introduction of EMI in higher education in Europe (Ammon & McConnell 2002; Wächter 2008). This special position of English is attested in the University of Helsinki Language Policy, where EMI is seen as one of the key elements in furthering international co-operation: "Developing and increasing the range of programmes taught in English is an integral part of creating an international learning environment" (UH Language Policy 2007: 43).

What does this international learning environment look like? With some exceptions, English-medium courses at the University of Helsinki are open to all students at the university, including degree students studying in English-medium programmes, exchange students, and domestic students not studying in the programmes. Exchange and domestic students go through different admission procedures compared to those applying for English-medium programmes. When applying for a degree programme, applicants are expected to pass a language test in English, which means that, already upon entering the programme, the selected applicants are expected to possess good enough skills in English to complete their degree (see Graduate admissions for the accepted tests and exemption criteria). Exchange students are also expected to prove their skills in English, but different rules apply (see Exchange student admissions). This means that students attending a course may have passed different types of language requirements. The resulting variation in the students' proficiency in and use of English is what the students and teachers need to cope with. This was also the reality in the course and group-work meetings focused on in this study: there was variation in the student status as well as the students' self-reports of their skills in English.[1] It should also be noted that teachers are not tested for their English skills, but rather it is left for the teachers themselves to evaluate whether they can teach in English or not.

Support in English is integrated in most of the English-medium degree programmes. This is in line with the university's Language Policy, which states that

> [t]eachers teaching in English and students studying in English-language programmes will be offered language support which aims to improve their ability to interact in English in a multicultural academic environment (UH Language Policy 2007:45).

The university is thus already tackling some of the concerns that the increase in the use of English in academia has caused (see Coleman 2006; Phillipson 2006). What is notable is that the language policy talks about the academic environment as "international" and "multicultural" and describes the aims to improve teachers' and students' ability to interact in English in relation to such an environment. This means that the policy advocates the training of English for the purposes of using it as a lingua franca. This study, with its focus on the micro-level of using ELF in EMI can be used to inform the current language-training practices.

The institute responsible for providing students (and staff) with language instruction is the Language Centre of the university (see LC). The Language Centre arranges courses in a range of different languages for students from all faculties, and offers custom-made language support in most English-medium degree programmes (see EM support). Through its Language Services unit the Language Centre also provides the personnel of the university with, for instance, courses on teaching in English, as well as translation and language revision services.

The English-language courses and support are meant for degree students only. The language support given in the degree programmes is mainly geared towards improving the students' academic writing skills in English, but some attention is put, for instance, on presentation skills. There is variation as regards the amount of support in English offered in the different programmes, whether it is obligatory for the students or not, and to what extent the support is integrated in the actual content classes; rather than offered as adjunct language (or academic writing) courses, as has been customary for courses in English for Specific Purposes (Räisänen & Fortanet-Gómez 2008:43).

In the course and group-work meetings focused on in this study, integrated language support on how to give a presentation in English was given in one group. All students in the group, irrespective of their student status, received comments from the English instructor attending the group-work meetings. Also, as will be shown in the Results section, language was taken up by the subject teachers and/or the students in the other groups as well, and thus became the focus of attention even if language support as such was not integrated in the groups' meetings. Individual students might also have personal motivations for learning English and, as Smit (2010) points out, it is plausible to suggest that language learning takes place, even if it may not be an official goal in itself.

Saarinen and Nikula's (2012) study focusing on descriptions for English-medium degree programmes in Finnish higher education institutions suggests that the programmes are not perceived as environments for language learning: the role of English remains marginal in the programme descriptions, and English skills are stated as a prerequisite for studying in the programme, rather than something to be developed during one's studies. While the English language requirements for degree students at the University of Helsinki suggest the same, EMI in the degree programmes can be seen as content-focused teaching, which, because of the integration of language support, illustrates "moves towards the adoption of CLIL [or rather, ICL]" (Coyle, Hood & Marsh 2010:26; my comment).[2] In addition, taking up language as a topic in actual course and group-work interaction (see Results section) sheds light on the micro-level integration of content and language in an EMI setting.

EMI as interaction in English as a lingua franca

In the EMI setting focused on in this study, English functioned as the students' and teachers' lingua franca, which by definition refers to a language used for communication between people who do not share a first language (L1). The students and teachers, then, are viewed primarily as users of English for whom the language is a common means of communication; and not as learners of English as a second or foreign language who seek to improve their language skills. Of course, integrated language support does place students in the position of language learners, and it is also possible that a speaker takes on the role of language learner, for instance, by referring to his or her English as inadequate. However, since the main purpose of EMI in the course and group-work meetings in this study was to discuss set themes and/or to prepare a joint presentation, English was a means of communication — not the object of study. Also, evaluation focused on the students' course and group-work performance, not their English skills. What thus becomes important is a focus on interaction in ELF.

Research has been conducted on different types of ELF interaction, ranging from academic to business and more casual settings (for an overview see Jenkins, Cogo & Dewey 2011; for academic ELF see Björkman 2011; Mauranen 2011). Previous studies where EMI in higher education has been approached as ELF interaction have looked into, for instance, the morphosyntax (Björkman 2008), pragmatics (Björkman 2009; Hynninen 2011; Knapp 2011a, 2011b; Smit 2009, 2010) and interactional features of EMI (Suviniitty forthcoming). In addition, studies on the ELFA corpus of English as an Academic Lingua Franca shed light on such ELF interaction (e.g. Mauranen 2006, 2007; Metsä-Ketelä 2006; Ranta 2006; see ELFA), although the corpus also includes other types of academic speech events than educational ones (e.g. conference presentations). ELF studies dealing with higher education have further looked into lecture comprehension (e.g. Airey 2009; Mulligan & Kirkpatrick 2000), and some also report on student and teacher views of EMI in international settings (e.g. Jensen & Thøgersen 2011; Pecorari et al. 2011; Smit 2010:121–147). The closest research focus to the one taken in this study is Smit (2010:ch 7), whose analysis on interactive explaining sheds light on language expertise in English-medium lectures.

Despite the increasing number of studies on ELF, and the central role of ELF interaction in higher education today, most of EMI/ICL in higher education research has not incorporated ELF research and its findings. This is surprising, because if we want to understand the situation in higher education today, we need to take into account the interactional settings in which teachers and students communicate. In international English-medium degree programmes, this means a focus on ELF. The present study can thus be seen as an attempt to build bridges between research on EMI/

ICL in higher education and ELF research. I do this by examining the micro-level of ELF interaction in EMI settings, particularly focusing on the construction of language expertise in such interaction.

Method

In this study, interaction in EMI settings is approached as interaction in ELF. The data come from English-medium course and group-work meetings, where English was not the subject of teaching, but rather the lingua franca used for in-group communication. In the following sections I describe the data collection and data analysis procedures.

Data collection

The data were collected for the purposes of a wider study on language regulation (Hynninen submitted), as part of the *Studying in English as a lingua franca* project at the University of Helsinki (see SELF). The data collection was ethnographically informed: naturally-occurring interactions in EMI settings were audio-recorded and observed, and students and teachers attending the events interviewed. In this study, however, I only draw on the interactions and their transcripts. The interactions were chosen based on three criteria: (1) English was a necessary lingua franca for in-group communication; (2) the interactions were polylogues, rather than monologues; and (3) the interactions came from different types of EMI settings, with different combinations of institutional speaker roles. For the purpose of analysing language expertise construction in ELF interaction, the key was to focus on more interactional contexts than lectures. In addition, I used different types of EMI settings in order to investigate what kind of effect institutional speaker roles may have on language expertise construction.

The data therefore consist of audio-recordings (in total ca. 20 h 35 min) and their transcripts of (a) interrelated group-work meetings of two discussion groups in the fields of biology and forestry, and (b) a course in the field of forestry. Both discussion groups aimed at preparing a joint presentation on a given topic. One discussion group was an all-student group with five students; the other also had five students, but was guided by two junior scholars who acted as the group's mentors. In addition, an English instructor visited the latter group for a short time on two occasions. In the course, students gave presentations (based on written reports) that were then discussed in class. The course had 11 students and two teachers. The students and mentors/teachers in these events represented different L1s (e.g. Arabic, Spanish and Finnish), and they thus used ELF. One student in both discussion groups and two students in the course were NSs of English.

Data analysis

A close analysis of language commenting and correcting was undertaken in order to explore the language expert roles adopted by the speakers in the ELF interaction. Overt language comments of both one's own and each other's language, that is, metalingual, rather than metadiscursive, comments (Berry 2005: 8–12) were taken into closer analysis. All metalingual comments were collected and classified according to who did the commenting, and if the commenting was allocated, who assigned the expert role to whom. Metalingual comments correspond to references to and comments on language (e.g. *what's that in English, when you are pronouncing the word*), which means that my focus is on those instances of the interaction where language is taken up as a topic. Metadiscourse, or talk about the talk itself (e.g. *as I said before, does this sound...to you*), is excluded from the analysis (for studies on metadiscourse, see e.g. papers in Ädel & Mauranen 2010).

In addition to metalingual commenting, the analysis focused on other corrections of language. All instances of corrections were collected and classified in terms of who initiated and who actually did the correcting. In Conversation Analysis, other corrections fall under the category of other repairs, which refers to those instances of interaction where participants temporarily stop the course of action in progress in order to solve some communicational 'trouble' (Brouwer, Rasmussen & Wagner 2004; Schegloff 1992; Schegloff, Jefferson & Sacks 1977; Schegloff et al. 2002). This means that only such instances are considered where the repair forms a side sequence in the interaction (cf. Jefferson 1987). Extract (1) illustrates the structure of a repair sequence. Transcription conventions are given at the end of this paper, and important bits in the extracts are marked with italics.

(1)   ⟨S4⟩ ((…)) they have different climatic conditions er ranging from (sahara) or semi-arid zone to the tropical zone where annual rainfall is er is 100 or 15000 millimetre annually but er [beekeeping] ⟨/S4⟩
⟨T1⟩ *[not 15000] 1000- er 1500* ⟨/T1⟩
⟨S4⟩ yeah 1500 yeah 1500 1000 and 500 millimetre annually but er it's still in separate areas scattered area(s) you will find bee practice beekeeping practice but ((…)) ⟨/S4⟩

In this extract, S4's presentation on beekeeping is interrupted by T1's repair (*not 15,000 1000- er 1500*). This is followed by S4 repeating the repaired item, after which he continues with the topic at hand. The repair thus forms a side sequence in the interaction. Extract (1) shows that repairs may or may not concern language, which makes the category too broad for my purposes. For this reason I have narrowed down the category of repairs to repairs dealing with language, that is, language corrections. Extract (1) is treated as a borderline case, since it deals with the contents of the presentation. At the same time, however, it is a correction of linguistic form and can thus be seen to have a dual function as a content repair and a language correction. In this study, along with language commenting, both other corrections of language (as in extract (1)) and corrections initiated by the speaker are included in the analysis in order to consider both the adoption and allocation of language expertise in ELF.

To sum up, I used the above criteria to isolate those instances of the interaction where speakers took on the role of language experts, and where expertise was allocated to an interlocutor. This was done to make the analysis as systematic as possible. After the classification of the metalingual comments and the language corrections, I analysed the instances for the kind of commenting and correcting done. Language commenting and correcting were chosen because they are explicit means of intervening in language during interaction, and thus represent clear instances of language expertise construction.

Results

Instances of metalingual commenting and/or language correcting were found in all of the group-work and course meetings, even if the scope and type of the metalingual comments and the corrections varied from meeting to meeting. Based on a close analysis of the metalingual comments and the corrections, I discerned four language expert roles in the data: (1) one based on subject expertise, which was related to a speaker's professional role and expertise in the relevant subject, (2) L1-based expertise, which means that the authority was allocated to a NS of English, (3) negotiation between speakers, where any of the speakers could do the commenting, and (4) expertise of the language professional, which means that an English instructor was treated as the language expert. Below, I analyse each of the categories in turn to consider what 'normative' authorities the speakers constructed as relevant in the interaction.

Subject teacher as the language expert
When language was commented on or corrected in the groups, it was mostly done by the teachers and mentors, who were sometimes asked to take on the role of language expert, but who also took

on the role themselves. Extract (2) illustrates how language was taken up as a topic even if it did not concern field-specific terminology. The extract comes from a discussion after a student's (S8) presentation.

(2) ⟨T2⟩ ((…)) could we take a few language questions here ⟨/T2⟩
⟨T1⟩ yes please ⟨/T1⟩
⟨T2⟩ er er ⟨NAME S8⟩ *correctly* used the the th- th- the name of the country as the sudan remember that this is the the name of the country the sudan like the gambia there are a few country names where you have the although the *modern usage* is (to omit it) the only thing you have to be con- consequent either you always say the sudan the sudan or then without the but there are this is one of the few country names where where it is ⟨/T2⟩
⟨BS2⟩ [so why (is it why is it)] ⟨/BS2⟩
⟨T2⟩ [er and th- the] government uses it's the republic of the sudan that's (the) *official name* of the country ⟨/T2⟩
⟨BS2⟩ so why do they use the ⟨/BS2⟩
⟨T2⟩ th- we you have to ask linguists there are er like the gambia (it) because it [refers to] ⟨/T2⟩
⟨T1⟩ [or the netherlands] ⟨/T1⟩
⟨T2⟩ what ⟨/T2⟩
⟨T1⟩ the netherlands ⟨/T1⟩
⟨T2⟩ jaa f- er plural names are natural you know why it is but er but er gambia it's because the river *rivers always have the* so that follows a- and sudan it there was something similar it was the sud was th- the wet area and then the sudan came from the sud probably this is the ⟨T1⟩ [mhm yeah okay] ⟨/T1⟩ [explanation] this is my my my understanding but it's also *correct* to say without the [nowadays] ⟨S2⟩ [mhm-hm] ⟨/S2⟩ especially *in scientific contexts* ⟨/T2⟩

In this extract, T2 takes an active role in suggesting language as a topic (*could we take a few language questions here*), after which he takes on the role of language expert by commenting on the 'correctness' of a country name used in a student's presentation and written report. We can see that the teacher expresses his internalised conception of the correct usage by referring to *modern usage* and usage *in scientific contexts* as opposed to the official name of the country and the grammar rule *rivers always have the*. There are thus two opposing forces at play in the teacher's comment: for one, the teacher draws on established standards, that is, the official name of the country, and the grammar rule generally taught in English language classes; but for another, his comment implies that usage in scientific contexts legitimises 'new' language norms. Of course, what is important is not whether the teacher is 'correct' in his understanding of the usage, but that he is ready to accept 'scientific contexts' as norm providing.

This can further be seen to mean that the teacher is leaning on his role as an expert in his field, rather than English; but on the basis of his experience of scientific contexts, he is confident enough to make the claim. This is evidence for the language expert role being based on the speaker's professional role and expertise in the relevant subject matter. It is also notable that the teacher took on the role of language expert even if he was a second language (L2) speaker of English[3] and even if he was not a language professional. Nor did he ask either of the two students who spoke English as an L1 in the group for help. Rather, extract (2) shows that one of the NSs of English (BS2, a native speaker of Twi and West-African English) is the one who poses T2 the question *so why do they use the*, which can be seen as a sign of acknowledging the teacher's authority on English.

As we can see in extracts (3) and (4), the students tended to turn to the teachers and mentors if they experienced trouble in expressing themselves. In extract (3), a student (S6) seeks help for a particular term during his presentation.

(3) ⟨S6⟩ ((…)) and this is er a very well this is like the typical the most typical plant in western sahara *i don't know the name* [(xx)] ⟨/S6⟩
     ⟨T2⟩ [(calotropis)] ⟨/T2⟩
     ⟨S6⟩ i ⟨/S6⟩
     ⟨T2⟩ (calotropis) ⟨/T2⟩
     ⟨S6⟩ okay *i knew that you could help (me) with this* and this erm this is erm a very important ((…)) ⟨/S6⟩
     ⟨T2⟩ the english name is dead sea apple dead sea apple is the [name] ⟨SU⟩ [mhm] ⟨/SU⟩ of the (calotropis in english). ⟨/T2⟩

The extract shows that we are dealing with terminology from the teacher's area of expertise, and that the teacher provides both the scientific and the English name of the plant (*calotropis, dead sea apple*) in question. The teacher's expertise in the subject matter thus ties in with language, similarly to what Smit (2010: 362–365) reports in her study. The extract (3) also illustrates the assignment of the language expert role to the teacher: we can see that the student expected the teacher to be able to help him (*I knew that you could help (me) with this*).

Similarly, extract (4) shows a mentor (M2) providing language help.

(4) ⟨S3⟩ i think er ⟨FINNISH⟩ suomen luonnonsuojeluliitto ⟨/FINNISH⟩ what's that in english ⟨/S3⟩
     ⟨M2⟩ i think it's the finnish association for nature conservation ⟨/M2⟩
     ⟨S3⟩ okay they they complained to EU couple of years ago i don't know was that any help or has EU decided anything ⟨/S3⟩

In this extract, a student (S3) asks for an English translation of a name of a Finnish association, which is later on provided by M2. We can see that S3 makes use of a partially shared language in the group,[4] which means that an English translation was needed for all the group members to be included. Such use of partially shared languages foregrounds the multilingual setting of the ELF encounters, and shows how different languages can become important in negotiating language expertise (see Smit 2010: 280–282, 367–370).

In short, language expertise based on subject expertise illustrates that in ELF settings, being a NS of English does not automatically transform into authority in language. Rather, the extracts show that students at times assigned language expertise to the teachers (and mentors), which means that they acknowledged the language expert role of the teachers. That the teachers were active in taking on the role of language expert further illustrates the agency of L2 speakers of English in the ELF settings — even if NSs of English were present.

NS of English as the language expert
Apart from the finding that subject expertise also brought with it some form of language expertise, the data also show allocation of the language expert role to NSs of English. However, such allocation was only done by the students. This is illustrated in extract (5), where a student (S3) expresses her wish that another student (NS5) in the group do the proof reading of the group's presentation slides. NS5 is a NS of Canadian English.

(5) ⟨S3⟩ and for example if you ⟨REFERS TO NS5⟩ check(ed) the language it (would) be easier to, speak (right) ⟨NS5⟩ mhm-hm ⟨/NS5⟩ like @right@ right way ⟨/S3⟩

The extract not only illustrates that the student allocates the role of language expert to a NS of English, but in doing so she also constructs the importance of 'correctness' (*speak (right)*), which she sees in relation to English spoken by the NS.

Extract (6) illustrates how a student with (American) English as an L1 was asked to help with spelling.

(6) ⟨S2⟩ er how do you write traditional knowledge ⟨/S2⟩
⟨S5⟩ knowledge ⟨/S5⟩
⟨S2⟩ mhm ⟨/S2⟩
⟨S5⟩ (xx) (how do you) ⟨/S5⟩
⟨S2⟩*(xx) how is it* ⟨*NAME NS3*⟩ *help (with english)* ⟨/S2⟩
⟨S5⟩ knowledge it's something like this [knowledge] ⟨/S5⟩
⟨S2⟩ [traditional] knowledge kn- K N ⟨/S2⟩
⟨NS3⟩ er O W, L E ⟨/NS3⟩
⟨S2⟩ E ⟨/S2⟩
⟨S5⟩ (xx) (D) yeah yeah ⟨/S5⟩
⟨NS3⟩ [yes] ⟨/NS3⟩

In the extract, S2 addresses NS3 (the NS of English in this group), but as we can see, S5 offers help first, and the three students end up spelling the word in collaboration. Even if the NS of English was assigned the role of language expert, there was thus some overlap with the third category of negotiated expertise, where anyone could take on the role of language expert (see below).

The extracts illustrate that NSs of English were used as language experts, and thus their NS status was constructed as relevant. What is notable, though, is that the assignment of language expertise to the students who spoke English as an L1 was only done by the students.

Negotiated language expertise
In addition to language expertise based on subject matter expertise and L1 status, the data also showed that expertise was negotiated among speakers. This means that the expert role could be taken on by anyone in the interaction and that any of the speakers could occasionally ask for help. The following extract (7) is a case where a mentor (M1) throws in a Finnish word in an attempt to get help from the groups' Finnish speakers (two students and the other mentor (M2) in the group spoke Finnish).

(7) ⟨M1⟩ alright so next time ⟨NAME S3⟩ is chairing (for) you at least (or) everybody needs pen and paper (but) @at least you you need to be prepared@ ⟨BACKGROUND NOISE⟩ and let's er try to make it ⟨FINNISH⟩ kunnianhimoinen ⟨/FINNISH⟩ ⟨/M1⟩
⟨M2⟩ ambitious ⟨/M2⟩
⟨SU-1⟩ ambitious ⟨/SU-1⟩
⟨M1⟩ ambitious but also try to keep in the schedule so like er like next session is very free discussion about whatever comes into your mind about saimaa seal but then we'll try to push into, whatever we find interesting to limit it so that we don't end up sitting here six times having interesting discussions but not getting anywhere ⟨/M1⟩

We can see in extract (7) that M2 and SU-1 step in with the English translation of the Finnish word, which is then accepted by M1 who repeats the translation. The floor was open for anyone to take on the language expert role, and we can see that two of the Finnish speakers do that (the other mentor and a student). We can thus treat this extract as a case of language expertise negotiation. The extract further demonstrates the multilingual nature of ELF encounters (see also extract 4), and the way speakers can draw on partially shared languages when need be. Negotiation can be seen as a means to ensure mutual understanding in the whole group — in extract (7), a translation was needed to include all group members.

Negotiation of language expertise also meant that a student could take on the expert role. This is the case in extract (8), where a student (S2) corrects another student (S5).

(8)   〈S2〉 and you have the this economics [er techniques] 〈/S2〉
       〈S5〉 [yeah (there) are economics] but of course er i haven't write i haven't numbers or a study yeah it's something like er (O) it's about O-N-G yeah O-N-G er 〈/S5〉
       〈S2〉 N-G-O 〈/S2〉
       〈S5〉 N-G-O yeah O-N-G is in spanish sorry 〈/S5〉
       〈S2〉 [(that's okay)] 〈/S2〉
       〈S5〉 [N-G-O yeah] N-G-O and er they have a lot of pages but of course nothing about er numbers. 〈/S5〉

The extract is a case of other correction where the correction is done without the speaker initiating the correction. The student doing the correcting was a NS of Brazilian Portuguese who reported to speak some Spanish, which may have helped her in deciphering the acronym that S5 used. It is also further evidence of the usefulness of partially shared languages (in this case Spanish) in ELF interaction (see Cogo & Dewey 2006; Hülmbauer 2009; Smit 2010: 280–282, 367–370).

Overall, the extracts of negotiation of language expertise showed that any of the speakers could occasionally ask for help, and that any of the speakers could act as the language expert. In general, it was rare for anyone to correct a mentor's or a teacher's language, although a few such instances did occur — mainly when initiated by the teacher or the mentor (see extract 7). The negotiation of language expertise illustrates that language expertise was not necessarily connected to subject expertise or one's status as a NS of English.

Language professional as the language expert
In addition to the three expert roles above, a fourth one, expertise of the language professional, could be found in one discussion group, where an English instructor paid two short visits to the group: the instructor attended the beginning of one of the group-work meetings to see how the group was doing, and he came to listen to and comment on the group's mock presentation. The instructor visited the group as part of the English language support offered to master's degree programmes by the Language Centre. His presence thus meant that the students had a dual role as members of the group and therefore users of ELF, *and* as learners of English monitored by the English instructor.

During the visits of the English instructor, there was a slight increase in the group's focus on language as the instructor was used as the main expert on language. This is illustrated in extract (9).

(9)   〈M1〉 i guess there's a sort of a problem er (what's) 〈FINNISH〉 jokamiehen oikeus 〈/FINNISH〉 〈/M1〉
       〈E1〉 everyman's [rights] 〈/E1〉
       〈S1〉 [everyman's] rights 〈/S1〉
       〈SU〉 [yeah] 〈/SU〉
       〈M1〉 [(xx)] (xx) in finland because (er) that's sort of if you completely 〈/M1〉

The English instructor (E1) was a NS of British English, but as the extract shows, he also spoke Finnish. Extract (9) is a typical case where E1 was drawn on as a dictionary. In the extract, a mentor (M1) requests for a translation of a Finnish phrase, which is followed by E1 taking on the language expert role by providing M1 with the requested translation. The extract further shows that one of the students (S1) was also ready to step in to provide the requested phrase in English, which illustrates negotiation of language expertise in the group. However, the English instructor was used as the main expert in language. This is not surprising in the sense that as an English instructor, he was also an institutionally appointed expert in language. What is notable, though, is that the instructor was allotted the role of language expert over the mentors and students in the group (including the English-NS student).

In his comments on the group's mock presentation, E1 commented on, for instance, pronunciation, as illustrated in extract (10).

(10) ⟨E1⟩ but one (other) thing ⟨NAME S4⟩ just to note that that when you're pronouncing the word cave if you try and keep it distinct ⟨S4⟩ yeah ⟨/S4⟩ you're saying (it) sometimes as as cove ⟨S4⟩ ah okay ⟨/S4⟩ and a cove is quite a different thing ⟨S4⟩ [@@] ⟨/S4⟩ [it's more like] an inlet like ⟨FINNISH⟩ ni- ⟨/FINNISH⟩ ⟨S4⟩ yeah yeah ⟨/S4⟩ ⟨FINNISH⟩ niemi ⟨/FINNISH⟩ in finnish ⟨/E1⟩[5]
⟨S4⟩ okay thank you ⟨/S4⟩

What the comment does is to foreground language issues in the group. E1's comment is directed at S4, a NS of Spanish, which means that his use of Finnish may only be explained by the presence of other group members who did speak Finnish.

The analysis therefore shows that the presence of an institutionally appointed language expert changed the nature of the interaction in that when the English instructor was present, the group tended to assign language expertise to him. The findings thus imply that an institutional authority overrode other language expert roles. Importantly, though, we saw that language was corrected and taken up as a topic in the form of metalingual comments also in those course and group-work meetings where the explicit focus was on content only.

Discussion and conclusions

We have provided evidence of the fact that language could be taken up as a topic by any of the speakers, but that the way this was done took different forms: Firstly, the teachers/mentors took on the role of language experts more actively than the students, and only the students assigned language expertise to NSs of English. Secondly, the presence of an English instructor influenced the assignment of expert roles. The findings show that language correcting and metalingual commenting were done in the groups even if the English instructor only attended one of the groups, and even if he only attended this one group occasionally. In fact, the data reveal that language expertise was primarily taken on by L2 speakers of English who were also experts in the subject matter taught (subject expertise). This means that the experts in the field to some extent shared their conceptions of (good) language use with their students, and in this sense integrated language to the content classes, even if learning English was not an official aim. This implies a connection between subject-matter expertise and willingness and ability to take on the role of language expert. This interpretation is supported by the students allocating the language expert role to their teachers as seen in extracts (3) and (4) above. This again reflects the students' role as novices in the field and as learners of the contents and conventions of that field, including those related to language use. That the students also turned to their fellow English-NS students for support in English (L1-based expertise) indicates that NSs of English were seen to possess expertise in English on the basis of their L1 status. The division between NSs and non-native speakers was thus constructed to matter, even if the main dividing line was between subject experts and novices, especially since the teachers did not rely on the English-NS students for expertise in English.

The findings to some extent correspond to those in Smit's research (2010: 362–365), where metalingual comments were found to be mainly subject-specific, and the teachers the experts relied on. For subject-related terminology, the teachers were the language experts in both studies. Smit (2010: 365–367) also shows that anyone could take on the role of language expert in order to help out with more general terms and expressions, which was the case with negotiated expertise in this study, too. That language expertise could be negotiated further supports Smit's (2010: 374) findings that asking for language help was not seen to diminish one's expertise in the topic itself. The difference between the two studies is, though, that in Smit (2010), there was a tendency to sign over language issues to language classes, as the following quote attests:

> Whenever the interaction turned to a language issue, it concerned the introduction or explanation of mainly subject-specific terms or expressions. Other aspects of language were not topicalized in any of the 33 lessons analysed in detail, or, if identified as an issue at all, were relegated to the English language classes. (Smit 2010: 408)

In this study, speakers used a wider range of metalingual comments, and language issues came to be integrated in the course and group-work meetings also when the explicit focus was on content only. What the speakers did when commenting and correcting language was to negotiate acceptable usage. The attention to language brought to light the usefulness of plurilingual resources in the negotiation process (extracts 4 and 7–9; see Smit 2010: 280–282, 367–370), and the explicit commenting and correcting further allowed incidental language learning to take place (e.g. terminology, but also what is acceptable usage in the field).

The differences between Smit's findings and those of this study may relate to the more interactive character of the course and group-work meetings in this study, as opposed to the lectures focused on in Smit (2010). In addition, the groups in this study also discussed written texts (presentation slides or reports). Written language tends to be more standardised than speech (see Milroy & Milroy 1985), and correcting and commenting on written language may thus be expected to be more straightforward. Indeed, language was more often taken up as a topic by the teachers in relation to students' written texts, although some correcting and commenting of spoken language also occurred.

The findings show that NSs of English participating in ELF interaction do not necessarily play a role as language experts, as demonstrated by the subject-expertise-based and negotiated language expertise. This is in contrast to studies of L1–L2 interaction, where it has been found that when correcting takes place, the majority of (if not all) corrections are done by L1 speakers who correct L2 speakers' language (Hosoda 2006; Kurhila 2003, contributions in Gardner & Wagner 2004). Hosoda (2006), in her study on casual L1–L2 conversations in Japanese, found that although by default language form was not oriented to, the L1 and L2 speakers did orient to NS status (or language expert vs. novice roles) at some occasions. She reports that other corrections were found to occur (a) when invited by an L2 speaker (e.g. by vocabulary check), and (b) when mutual understanding was at stake (Hosoda 2006). Similarly, Kurhila's (2003) study on institutional L1–L2 talk in Finnish shows that in the L1–L2 interaction, other corrections were not common, but when they occurred, they were exclusively done by a NS of Finnish. Although the L1–L2 interactions in the two studies mentioned are not directly comparable to the ELF interaction explored in this study, they do imply the importance of NS status in L1–L2 interaction; whereas the findings of this study point towards a reduced importance of the status in ELF interaction, and an increased importance of subject matter expertise.[6]

The agency of L2 speakers of English in acting as language experts in this study further means that the findings cast doubt on the NS ownership of English (see Haberland 2011; Widdowson 1994). The question of ownership is central in terms of deciding who can take on the role of language expert, and thus decide on the norms others are supposed to follow. The traditional view has been that NSs of English are (or should be) the sole owners of English (Quirk 1990; Trudgill 2002), whereas some scholars argue that ownership can also be claimed by L2 users of English: by speakers of postcolonial varieties (Kachru 1996), and also by speakers of ELF (Jenkins 2000; Seidlhofer 2011). The central question is, of course, what speakers do in interaction. If speakers in ELF interaction grant the ownership to NSs of English, they will continue using NSs of English (and standards of English as a native language) to measure the acceptability and accuracy of their usage, which means a reliance on exonormative standards. Then again, that L2 speakers in this study were found to take on the role of language experts is a step towards endonormativity.

To sum up, this paper has contributed to the aims of the present *AILA Review* volume on ICL in European higher education by providing a micro-level perspective on interaction in EMI settings. We have seen that language was taken up as a topic in the course and group-work meetings even when an English instructor was not present. In this sense, principles of ICL were adopted at the level of interaction also when learning English was not an official aim of the course or group work. The extent to which language was focused on depended on the initiatives of the students and teachers, as well as their willingness to take on the role of experts in English. When language correcting and metalingual commenting took place, it allowed incidental language learning to occur: not only in terms of field-specific terminology, but also in terms of insider views of the language use in the field.

By focusing on language expert roles observable in ELF interaction, this study has illustrated the diversity of possible roles and the multitude of 'normative' authorities speakers may draw on. The findings can thus be interpreted as suggesting that determining who can act as language authority or which language norms and standards are relevant for the speakers is not pre-determined, but rather negotiated in interaction. Specifically, this kind of investigation sheds light on the negotiation process: the construction of relevance or irrelevance of NS status and of codified language standards in interaction. For instance, that subject-matter expertise and taking on the role of language expert were often found to go together suggests the importance of disciplinary literacy over NS status. This observation supports taking disciplinary literacy as the guiding principle of teaching academic English. In general, the findings can be used to focus the teaching of (academic) English on aspects relevant for international communication.

Acknowledgments

I would like to express my warmest thanks to all the students and teachers who participated in this study, as well as to the project assistants who helped me in the collection and transcription of the data. My thanks also go to the guest editors of this volume, Emma Dafouz and Ute Smit, as well as the anonymous reviewers for their support and valuable comments on earlier drafts of this paper. This study has benefited from funding from the Studying in English as a lingua franca (SELF) project (funded by the University of Helsinki Research Funds 2008–2010), the Global English (GlobE) project (funded by the Academy of Finland 2010–2012) and the Langnet doctoral programme.

Notes

1. I have conducted research interviews with a number of the students. With the students' self-reports I refer to the accounts they gave in the interviews. The interviews are discussed in Hynninen (2010; submitted).

2. The two terms Content and Language Integrated Learning (CLIL) and ICL are often used interchangeably, but there is a tendency to favour CLIL when talking about primary and secondary education and ICL when talking about tertiary education (Gustafsson et al. 2011). Because of the specificities of EMI at tertiary level such as the diverse language backgrounds of the students and teachers (see Smit 2010: 43–44; see also Smit & Dafouz, this volume), the concept adopted in this study is ICL.

3. With L2, I refer to any language a person speaks in addition to his or her L1, be it his or her second, third etc. language.

4. In this particular group-work meeting, only two students and one mentor were present. One student spoke German as an L1, and S3 and M2 were Finnish speakers.

5. An 'inlet' would actually translate as 'salmi' or 'lahti', and a 'cape' as 'niemi'.

6. However, compare Zuengler (1993), who has shown that subject matter expertise does influence the dynamics of L1–L2 interaction, too.

References

Ädel, A. & Mauranen, A. (eds) 2010. *Nordic Journal of English Studies* 9(2). *Special Issue on Metadiscourse.*
Airey, J. 2009. Science, language and literacy: Case studies of learning in Swedish university physics. Unpublished PhD thesis. Uppsala University, ⟨http://uu.diva-portal.org/smash/record.jsf?pid=diva2:173193⟩ (22 May 2012).
Ammon, U. & McConnell, G. 2002. *English as an Academic Language in Europe: A Survey of Its Use in Teaching.* Frankfurt: Peter Lang.
Berry, R. 2005. Making the most of metalanguage. *Language Awareness* 14(1): 3–20.
Björkman, B. 2008. English as the Lingua Franca of engineering: The morphosyntax of academic speech events. *Nordic Journal of English Studies* 7(3): 103–122.
Björkman, B. 2009. From code to discourse in spoken ELF. In *English as a Lingua Franca: Studies and Findings*, A. Mauranen & E. Ranta (eds), 225–251. Newcastle upon Tyne: Cambridge Scholars Publishing.
Björkman, B. 2011. English as a lingua franca in higher education: Implications for EAP. *Ibérica* 22: 79–100.
Bologna Process. The Bologna Process — building a European Higher Education Area, ⟨http://www.coe.int/t/dg4/highereducation/EHEA2010/Default_en.asp⟩ (22 May 2012).
Brouwer, C. E.; Rasmussen, G. & Wagner, J. 2004. Embedded corrections in second language talk. In *Second Language Conversations*, R. Gardner & J. Wagner (eds), 75–92. London: Continuum.
Canagarajah, S. 2006. Changing communicative needs, revised assessment objectives: Testing English as an international language. *Language Assessment Quarterly* 3(3): 229–242.
Cogo, A. & Dewey, M. 2006. Efficiency in ELF communication: From pragmatic motives to lexico-grammatical innovation. *Nordic Journal of English Studies* 5(2): 59–93, ⟨http://hdl.handle.net/2077/3148⟩ (22 May 2012).
Coleman, J.A. 2006. English-medium teaching in European higher education. *Language Teaching* 39(1): 1–14.
Coyle, D., Hood, P. & Marsh, D. 2010. *CLIL: Content and Language Integrated Learning.* Cambridge: Cambridge University Press.
ELFA. ELFA Corpus of English as an Academic Lingua Franca, ⟨http://www.helsinki.fi/elfa/elfacorpus⟩ (22 May 2012).
EM support. Support for English-medium master's programmes at the University of Helsinki, ⟨http://h27.it.helsinki.fi/emkt/support_needs.html⟩ (22 May 2012).
Exchange student admissions. Application information for exchange students applying to the University of Helsinki. Language requirements, ⟨http://www.helsinki.fi/exchange/howtoapply/index.html#LanguageRequirements⟩ (22 May 2012).

Gardner, R. & Wagner, J. (eds) 2004. *Second Language Conversations*. London: Continuum.

Graddol, D. 2006. *English Next. Why Global English May Mean the End of 'English as a Foreign Language'*. British Council.

Graduate admissions. Graduate admissions of the University of Helsinki. Language requirements, ⟨http://www.helsinki.fi/admissions/language_skills.htm⟩ (22 May 2012).

Gustafsson, M., Eriksson, A., Räisänen, C., Stenberg, A.-C., Jacobs, C., Wright, J., Wyrley-Birch, B. & Winberg, C. 2011. Collaborating for content and language integrated learning: The situated character of faculty collaboration and student learning. *Across the Disciplines* 8(3), ⟨http://wac.colostate.edu/atd/clil/index.cfm⟩ (22 May 2012).

Haberland, H. 2011. Ownership and maintenance of a language in transnational use: Should we leave our lingua franca alone? *Journal of Pragmatics* 43(4): 937–949.

Hosoda, Y. 2006. Repair and relevance of differential language expertise in second language conversations. *Applied Linguistics* 27(1): 25–50.

Hülmbauer, C. 2009. We don't take the right way. We just take the way we think you will understand — The shifting relationship between correctness and effectiveness in ELF. In *English as a Lingua Franca: Studies and Findings*, A. Mauranen & E. Ranta (eds), 323–347. Newcastle upon Tyne: Cambridge Scholars Publishing.

Hynninen, N. 2010. "We try to to to speak all the time in easy sentences" — Student conceptions of ELF interaction. *Helsinki English Studies* 6: 29–43, ⟨http://blogs.helsinki.fi/hes-eng/volumes/volume-6⟩ (22 May 2012).

Hynninen, N. 2011. The practice of 'mediation' in English as a lingua franca interaction. *Journal of Pragmatics* 43(4): 965–977.

Hynninen, N. submitted. Language regulation in English as a lingua franca. Unpublished PhD thesis. University of Helsinki.

Jefferson, G. 1987. On exposed and embedded correction in conversation. In *Talk and Social Organisation*, G. Button & J.R.E. Lee (eds), 86–100. Bristol: Multilingual Matters.

Jenkins, J. 2000. *The Phonology of English as an International Language*. Oxford: Oxford University Press.

Jenkins, J., Cogo, A. & Dewey, M. 2011. Review of developments in research into English as a lingua franca. *Language Teaching* 44 (3): 281–315.

Jensen, C. & Thøgersen, J. 2011. Danish university lecturers' attitudes towards English as the medium of instruction. *Ibérica* 22: 13–34.

Kachru, B.B. 1996. Opening borders with World Englishes: Theory in the classroom. In *On JALT96. Crossing Borders. The Proceedings of the JALT 1996 International Conference on Language Teaching and Learning*, S. Cornwell, P. Rule & T. Sugino (eds), 10–20.

Knapp, A. 2011a. Using English as a lingua franca for (mis-)managing conflict in an international university context: An extract from a course in engineering. *Journal of Pragmatics* 43(4): 978–990.

Knapp, A. 2011b. When comprehension is crucial: Using English as a medium of instruction at a German university. In *English in Europe Today: Sociocultural and Educational Perspectives*, A. de Houver & A. Wilton (eds), 51–70. Amsterdam: John Benjamins.

Kurhila, S. 2003. Co-constructing understanding in second language conversation. Unpublished PhD thesis. University of Helsinki.

LC. The University of Helsinki Language Centre, ⟨http://www.helsinki.fi/kksc/english/index.html⟩ (22 May 2012).

Mauranen, A. 2006. Signalling and preventing misunderstanding in English as lingua franca communication. *International Journal of the Sociology of Language* 177: 123–150.

Mauranen, A. 2007. Hybrid voices: English as the lingua franca of academics. In *Language and Discipline Perspectives on Academic Discourse*, K. Flottum, T. Dahl & T. Kinn (eds), 244–259. Cambridge: Cambridge Scholars Publishing.

Mauranen, A. 2011. English as the lingua franca of the academic world. In *New Directions in English for Specific Purposes Research*, D. Belcher, A.M. Johns & B. Paltridge (eds), 94–117. Ann Arbor: Michigan University Press.

Metsä-Ketelä, M. 2006. "Words are more or less superfluous": The case of more or less in academic lingua franca English. *Nordic Journal of English Studies* 5(2): 117–143.

Milroy, J. & Milroy, L. 1985. *Authority in Language. Investigating Language Prescription and Standardisation.* London: Routledge.

Mulligan, D. & Kirkpatrick, A. 2000. How much do they understand? Lectures, students and comprehension. *Higher Education Research & Development* 19(3): 311–335.

Pecorari, D., Shaw, P., Irvine, A. & Malmström, H. 2011. English for academic purposes at Swedish universities: Teachers' objectives and practices. *Ibérica* 22: 55–78.

Phillipson, R. 2006. English, a cuckoo in the European higher education nest of languages? *European Journal of English Studies* 10(1): 13–32.

Quirk, R. 1990. Language varieties and standard language. *English Today* 6(1): 3–10.

Räisänen, C. & Fortanet-Gómez, I. 2008. The state of ESP teaching and learning in Western European higher education after Bologna. In *ESP in European Higher Education: Integrating Language and Content*, I. Fortanet-Gómez & C.A. Räisänen (eds), 11–51. Amsterdam: John Benjamins.

Ranta, E. 2006. The 'attractive' progressive — Why use the -ing form in English as a lingua franca? *Nordic Journal of English Studies* 5(2): 95–116.

Saarinen, T. & Nikula, T. 2012. Implicit policy, invisible language: Policies and practices of international degree programmes in Finnish higher education. In *English-Medium Instruction at Universities. Global Challenges*, A. Doiz, D. Lasagabaster & J.M. Sierra (eds), 131–150. Multilingual Matters.

Schegloff, E.A. 1992. Repair after next turn: The last structurally provided defence of intersubjectivity in conversation. *American Journal of Sociology* 97(5): 1295–1345.

Schegloff, E.A., Jefferson, G. & Sacks, H. 1977. The preference for self correction in the organization of repair in conversation. *Language* 54: 361–382.

Schegloff, E.A., Koshik, I.M., Jacoby, S. & Olsher, D. 2002. Conversation analysis and applied linguistics. *Annual Review of Applied Linguistics* 22: 3–31.

Seidlhofer, B. 2009. Common ground and different realities: World Englishes and English as a lingua franca. *World Englishes* 28(2): 236–245.

Seidlhofer, B. 2011. *Understanding English as a Lingua Franca.* Oxford: Oxford University Press.

SELF. *Studying in English as a lingua franca* project. University of Helsinki. Director A. Mauranen, ⟨http://www.helsinki.fi/elfa/self⟩ (22 May 2012).

Smit, U. 2009. Emic evaluations and interactive processes in a classroom community of practice. In *English as a Lingua Franca: Studies and Findings*, A. Mauranen & E. Ranta (eds), 200–224. Newcastle upon Tyne: Cambridge Scholars Publishing.

Smit, U. 2010. *English as a Lingua Franca in Higher Education. A Longitudinal Study of Classroom Discourse.* Berlin: De Gruyter.

Suviniitty, J. forthcoming. Lectures in English as a lingua franca: Interactional features. Unpublished PhD thesis. University of Helsinki.

Trudgill, P. 2002. *Sociolinguistic Variation and Change.* Edinburgh: Edinburgh University Press.

UH Language Policy, 2007. University of Helsinki Language Policy. University of Helsinki. Administrative Publications 45. Strategies and Plans. 14 March 2007, ⟨http://www.helsinki.fi/strategia/pdf/HY_2007_kieliperiaatteet.pdf⟩ (22 May 2012).

Wächter, B. 2008. Teaching in English on the rise in European higher education. *International Higher Education* 52: 3–4, ⟨http://www.bc.edu/research/cihe/ihe/issues/2008.html⟩ (22 May 2012).

Widdowson, H. 1994. The ownership of English. *TESOL Quarterly* 28(2): 377–389.

Zuengler, J. 1993. Encouraging learners' conversational participation: The effect of content knowledge. *Language Learning* 43(3): 403–432.

Appendix: Transcription conventions

The transcriptions are based on a slightly modified version of the ELFA corpus transcription guide (see http://www.helsinki.fi/elfa). Special symbols used in this study are explained below.

Speaker codes:

⟨S#⟩	Student
⟨NS#⟩	Student (NS of English)
⟨BS#⟩	Student (bilingual speaker with English as one of the L1s)
⟨T#⟩	Teacher
⟨M#⟩	Mentor
⟨E#⟩	English instructor
⟨SU-#⟩	Uncertain speaker identification

Transcription symbols:

⟨S#⟩⟨/S#⟩	Utterance begins/ends
,	Brief pause 2–3 sec.
.	Pause 3–4 sec.
te-	Unfinished utterances
[text 1] [text 2]	Overlapping speech (approximate, shown to the nearest word, words not split by overlap tags)
(text)	Uncertain transcription
(xx)	Unintelligible speech
@@	Laughter
@text@	Spoken laughter
⟨NAME S#⟩	Names of participants in the same speech event
⟨FINNISH⟩⟨/FINNISH⟩	Code-switched elements (language specified in the tags)
⟨TEXT⟩	Descriptions and comments
((…))	Omitted text from transcription

Author's affiliation and e-mail address

Stockholm University, Sweden and University of Helsinki, Finland

niina.hynninen@english.su.se

Focus on form in ICLHE lectures in Italy

Evidence from English-medium science lectures by native speakers of Italian

Francesca Costa

This paper seeks to provide insights into the local context of ICLHE (Integrating Content and Language in Higher Education) in Italy. Its principal aim is descriptive although it also discusses theoretical models since it seeks to establish the extent to which Focus on Form (FonF) is present in ICLHE lectures. By means of observations, recordings and transcriptions, data were obtained from Italian university lecturers teaching in their scientific fields and using English as medium of instruction. The analysis of the results reveals a type of pre-emptive FonF on the part of the lecturers (namely, code-switching) which is rarely presented as such in the literature. Finally, the results furnish a pedagogical perspective, with evidence that content lecturers make certain use of FonF, thus revealing some degree of linguistic interest and awareness which could be further enhanced through the support of the language academic staff and which should be taken into consideration when designing training courses for university-level education.

Introduction

Since the beginning of the Bologna Process in 1999, and in some cases even earlier, European universities have had to deal with a series of challenges regarding how to better manage a world that is becoming increasingly globalised. Many universities in non-English speaking countries have thus decided to offer courses taught through English in some disciplines in order to be more competitive. Italy is one of these countries.

The choice of Italy for this research is connected to the boom in ICLHE (Integrating Content and Language in Higher Education) programmes in the past ten years. Italy, one of the largest countries in Southern Europe and one with a long university tradition dating back to the Middle Ages, has adapted to this new international situation, as testified by a specific section on internationalisation included in a new Italian law for universities (Legge Gelmini 240/2010), which strongly suggests a broadening of study programmes in a foreign language.

Despite this context, no study has so far focussed in depth on the situation in Italy, and even when taking Southern European countries more generally into account, research has been scarce and restricted to some Spanish universities (Fortanet 2008, this volume). More particularly, lecturing discourse in English in ICLHE settings and the teaching practices involved have only been dealt with in a single paper that concerns Italy (Veronesi 2009), while one research project has been undertaken in the Spanish context (e.g. Dafouz 2011; Dafouz, Nuñez, Sancho & Foran 2007). However, none of these have dealt with Focus on Form.

AILA Review 25 (2012), 30–47. DOI 10.1075/aila.25.03cos
ISSN 1461–0213 / E-ISSN 1570–5595 © John Benjamins Publishing Company

The present article, which is part of a broader study undertaken on ICLHE in Italy (Costa & Coleman 2012), proposes a micro-level analysis of lecturers' discursive attention to language as the vehicle for content in the context of six Italian lecturers from three different universities. The purpose of this study is thus firstly to provide the research community with information on ICLHE in Italy, as this has been found scarce (Pérez-Cañado 2012). Secondly, it aims to contribute to the further development of the continually evolving research into Focus on Form (cf. Ellis, Basturkmen & Loewen 2001), with Focus on Form being understood here as the level of attention to language on the part of lecturers of scientific subjects teaching through English at several Italian universities. In other words, this descriptive study contributes to this volume in two ways: firstly, it supplies data at the local level on how ICLHE lessons in Italy are carried out and, secondly, it makes a contribution to applied linguistics by analysing the discourse of vehicular teaching at the university level as well as by revisiting theoretical models. In particular, Focus on Form (FonF) is used in this paper as the framework for the linguistic analysis of lectures in order to understand to what extent such teaching could be viewed within the ICLHE (where the integration between language and content is explicit) or the EMI (English-medium Instruction) frameworks.

The paper begins with a terminological discussion of English-taught programmes, to be followed by a description of the context in question, an *excursus* on FonF, a presentation of the aims guiding the study reported and methodology used, and, finally, the presentation and discussion of the results.

The integration of content and language

The context of this study can be viewed in two ways: English as the Medium of Instruction (EMI) or Integrating Content and Language in Higher Education (ICLHE) (for a discussion see Smit & Dafouz's introduction to this volume). Even if 'English' forms an explicit part of the former acronym but not the latter, ICLHE often involves English as well. Moreover, the ICL acronym implies and suggests an integration of language and content, which it shares with the CLIL (Content and Language Integrated Learning) approach that is prototypically concerned with the teaching-learning process in schools, rather than at universities (but see some earlier references to tertiary CLIL, e.g. Dafouz, Nuñez & Sancho 2007; Greere & Räsänen 2008). It thus seems that the difference between the two terms (ICLHE and CLIL) is linked to the context in which the programme is carried out as well as the respective groups of teachers and students.

Despite the different conceptualizations at hand (ICL, EMI and CLIL), universities in Italy tend to define such courses more as English-taught programmes than as ICLHE ones. Nonetheless, insider views, such as the one given by a lecturer involved in the present study, reveal the *de facto* twofold aim of integrating both didactic aspects (language and content):

> this is why (.) just-just we decided to put the course in-in English language (.) just to have the possibility to host (3.0) eh eh eh student coming from abroad and give our students the possibility to learn a foreign language

As, additionally, English is employed as medium of instruction because of its fundamental value to today's working society (Coleman 2006), it is safe to conclude that the objective of such university programmes is not only to transmit content-based information but also to promote and implement the knowledge of English. In other words, this type of experience might be called ICLHE, as both areas (language and content) represent teaching objectives and are to some extent integrated. Therefore, ICLHE will be used as the term of reference in the following. Furthermore, the Focus on Form (FonF) analytical paradigm has been employed since it is one way of overcoming the separation of content and language (Lyster 2007).

Lecturers that adopt ICLHE in Italy are mainly non-native English-speaking content lecturers. Therefore, they are educationally disposed to teaching content over language. In fact, since a university course involves a degree of complexity and specialisation regarding the subject taught, lecturers are often prepared in terms of content but less so in terms of language. In this line, Dafouz (2011) studied physics lectures in Spain and found that they revealed a dichotomy between content and language issues: specifically, the subject-matter lecturers saw content as more important and language as not being part of their job. As, furthermore, content lecturers were not given any ICLHE training they felt inadequately prepared to handle language issues (cf. also Fortanet-Gómez 2010). In the same vein, Wilkinson (2004) notes the high risk of reducing the language aspect to a purely instrumental use, with no representation in the actual teaching context.

The Italian context

Italian universities, which are for the most part public institutions, are open to all students who have finished secondary school. With regard to levels of prestige, the most important criterion arguably is geographical location, with Northern universities thought to be more internationally competitive (Costa & Coleman 2012).

English-taught programmes were first introduced in universities in 1992. While there was a constant growth in such programmes throughout the '90s, a true acceleration began in 2004, as evidenced by a specific section on internationalisation included in the new law on universities (Legge Gelmini 240/2010), which clearly calls for more mobility among lecturers and students, more cooperation among universities regarding study and research, and the initiation of teaching or study programmes in foreign languages. Presently, most of such programmes are at the master's level, followed by the doctoral and bachelor's level (Costa & Coleman 2012; Wächter & Maiworm 2008).

Students and lecturers are for the most part native Italian speakers, there are almost no training courses for ICLHE lecturers, and university lectures still mainly take the form of lecturer monologues (Costa & Coleman 2012; Ricci Garotti 2009) although the use of English as the language of instruction seems to lower the teacher–student asymmetry even in this type of lecture (Veronesi 2009). Of interest in Veronesi's study, undertaken at the Free University of Bozen/Bolzano, is the use of code-switching, which revealed varied patterns, in that some lecturers practised it and others did not, perhaps because code-switching can be viewed as causing some loss of face by indicating inadequate linguistic competence on the part of the lecturer. The predominately monologic lecture is common to at least one other Southern European country, as testified by studies carried out in Spain (Dafouz 2007; Dafouz, Núñez & Sancho 2007; Dafouz Milne & Núñez Perucha 2010).

The role of the input and focus on form: proposed taxonomy

Subject-matter teaching using L2 in CLIL-like contexts has gained increasing recognition as it exposes learners to comprehensible input (Gass & Madden 1985; Krashen 1985). This approach uses content classes as the language input for learners. According to Krashen (1985), learners must first be exposed to linguistic structures slightly beyond their competence (i + 1) in order for language acquisition to take place. For him, language acquisition is a subconscious process that is different from learning, which is a conscious process. His theory views the objective of the teacher (who in his view should be a subject-matter teacher) as facilitating comprehension, to which end he/she produces language in order to convey content.

Long (1996) has gone further with Krashen's input theory, stating that interaction and negotiation of meaning play a very important role in SLA. Negotiation of meaning is to be understood as a way of overcoming obstacles in communication, and it is carried out by those involved in conversation. His theory was subsequently developed to include and combine focus on meaning and Focus on Form (Long & Robinson 1998). Ellis, Basturkmen and Loewen (2001:412–413) describe focus on meaning as "treat[ing] language as a tool for achieving some non-linguistic goal rather than as an object to be studied for the purposes of learning the language".

Focus on Form[1] encompasses moments in which

> the participants momentarily abandon using language as a tool in order to treat it as an object. We believe that such behaviour is quite normal for adult, motivated learners, who quite naturally look for opportunities to learn about form even in activities that are meaning centred (Ellis, Basturkmen & Loewen 2001:426).

Focus on Form, which is contrasted with Focus on Forms (i.e. teaching mainly the structures of a foreign language) is thus pivotal in higher education, arguably representing the way by which EMI becomes ICLHE.

Form-focused instruction can include elements of phonology, grammar, lexis and pragmatics (Pérez-Vidal 2007:47). As far as lexis is concerned, it can be described as a moment when the teacher abandons the activity on meaning in order to deal with lexis "as objects whose meaning can be learned". In other words, "explicit attention to the meanings of specific lexical forms in the context of meaning-focused activity constitutes focus on form" (Ellis, Basturkmen & Loewen 2001:415–416). Pavesi and Zecca (2001) observe that in CLIL contexts the attention is on the teaching of specific lexis both incidentally and through focusing on form (FonF). Thus, moments during which a term is explained are to be considered FonF (Ellis 2001).

In particular, regarding the corpus of this study, even the explanations of technical terms are considered FonF moments (language as an object). Nation (2001:204) supports this position, stating that "[c]onsidering the large numbers of technical words that occur in specialised texts, language teachers need to prepare learners to deal with them". If language teachers need to deal with them, then they can be considered activities where language is the object of learning (Focus on Form).

The dichotomy between FonF and focus on meaning can be interpreted in many ways (Loewen 2011); in fact, Seedhouse (1997) states that it is very difficult to draw a demarcation line between the two events. In ICLHE, the dichotomy can be likened at the macro level to the adjunct model (Brinton, Snow & Wesche 1989), where students can follow a content course at the same time they are following a support course whose focus is on language forms. At the micro level the dichotomy can also be carried out by the lecturers themselves within the same lecture. ICLHE contexts, which are inextricably intertwined with meaning, can represent the ideal occasion to promote FonF, understood as occasional moments of linguistic focus (language as an object) within more general moments focused on content (meaning as an object — language as a vehicle).

Furthermore, FonF in ICLHE contexts can lead to a so-called counterbalanced approach (Lyster 2007), where there is equilibrium between content-focused and form-focused teaching, which should lead to more effective input (Coonan 2007). FonF appears to be an important category of analysis since it indicates how much attention to language exists in meaning-focused teaching such as ICLHE. In this sense, it appears to be the acid test and meeting point for the integration of language and content in contexts where the lecturers are mainly subject lecturers and thus view themselves as subject specialists rather than language teachers (Aguilar & Rodríguez 2012; Costa in press; Dafouz 2011; see also Smit & Dafouz, this volume).

So far, few studies have investigated the extent to which FonF is present in ICLHE or CLIL contexts. Instead, several studies have concentrated on corrective feedback or repair as a reactive FonF especially in primary and secondary levels (Dalton-Puffer 2007; Mariotti 2006; Serra 2007). Pérez-Vidal (2007) performed a study in several CLIL primary and secondary school classes, noting no instance of Focus on Form.

Pre-emptive Focus on Form (lexical and grammatical)
As far as this study is concerned, the data have shown the presence only of the so-called pre-emptive FonF. In the literature, pre-emptive FonF is sometimes referred to as implicit or incidental, the latter being identified as "the incidental attention that teachers and L2 learners pay to form in the context of meaning-focussed instruction" (Ellis, Basturkmen & Loewen 2001:407). Moreover, Long (1991:46) states that FonF "overtly draws students' attention to linguistic elements as they arise incidentally in lessons whose overriding focus is on meaning, or communication". This type of FonF can also be called *implicit*, i.e. it "attracts attention to target form, is delivered spontaneously, is unobtrusive, presents target forms in context, makes no use of metalanguage" (Housen & Pierrard 2005:10).

Over time the concept has been broadened. Pre-emptive FonF represents "occasions when either the teacher or a student chose to make a specific form the topic of the discourse" (Ellis, Basturkmen & Loewen 2001:407). This could be called teacher-initiated FonF, which does not arise from a student error but from the teacher who, through his experience and intuition (Ellis 2001), understands that there is a problem. Pre-emptive FonF can involve grammatical, lexical, phonological items, but in the case of this study only grammatical and lexical instances were found. Moreover, along with lexical and grammatical FonF two other types of pre-emptive use have been added: input enhancement and code-switching (see Figure 1 and following paragraphs).

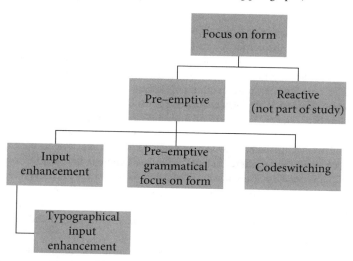

Figure 1. Taxonomy of FonF used for this study

In his work on FonF Van Patten (2009) analyses input enhancement or enhanced input, defined as a technique to get students' attention and thus support learning in meaning-focused contexts. In fact, metalinguistic awareness may be furthered by formal instruction, which can turn out to be useful for SLA (Sharwood Smith 1993). Along these lines, Sharwood Smith believes there are different types of input enhancement which are extremely important in formal instruction, in particular as a spur to language development in learners that have difficulty progressing to the next level, thus giving rise to discrepancies between the known linguistic system and the new one being presented (Gass 1997). It is interesting to note that Sharwood Smith (1993) uses the term input enhancement rather than consciousness raising, since the former does not draw any inferences about the effect of the input on the learner but simply implies that the input is somehow made more visible to the learner. Input, thus, can be of many types, one of which is typographical input enhancement (White 1998). With respect to this categorisation, input enhancement is also included within implicit or pre-emptive form-focused instruction.

Code-switching as a type of FonF was included in the proposed taxonomy only after the data revealed that the lecturers had used it to explain and translate lexis or whole expressions and as such, showed features that could be ascribed to pre-emptive FonF (see Figure 1). Several studies have dealt directly with code-switching in bilingual contexts, but only one has treated it in an ICLHE con-text (Myers 2008). All these studies promote code-switching[2] as a valid and natural learning strategy (e.g. Cook 2001), fitting to the present-day understanding of code-switching as fulfilling specific communicational aims, such as emphasising, substitution of words, saying something which cannot be expressed any other way, reinforcing a request, explaining, expressing identity, lightening the conversation, and excluding other people (Baker 2006).

In a study on bilingualism in Maltese schools Camilleri (1995: 129) found that code-switching was used to "explain or translate English terms, to enhance teachers' elicitation techniques and to establish rapport with learners". Camilleri also reported instances of terminology switching, which she divided into: technical terms, sub-technical terms, classroom jargon, numerical expressions and non-technical terms. Butzkamm's research (1998) in bilingual contexts concluded that scientific terms should also be taught in the L1, since code-switching is a key competence of bilinguals and, if used appropriately and systematically, constitutes a natural support. In the same vein, Gajo (2001) underlined a difference between micro-alternance and macro-alternance: the former occurs when teachers switch from one language to another within the same verbal interaction, while the latter takes place when they decide to teach all or part of a discipline in the L2. Micro-alternance indicates bilingual competence, since it is common knowledge that bilinguals frequently switch from one language to the other.

Against this theoretical backdrop, the research questions guiding the study are:

a.   To what extent is FonF *present* in the lecture discourse of native speaking Italian lecturers when teaching in English?
b.   What *types* of FonF are present in the lecture discourse of these speakers?

Method

A qualitative paradigm (Creswell 1998; Marshall & Rossman 1994) has been chosen for this study since it aims at investigating a social problem based on observation and has proved to be effective when conducted in educational settings such as universities. Its aim is to analyse lecturers' discourse; it does not seek to define the outcomes but is based totally on field work, using the researcher her-self (who is also the author of the study) as the main investigative instrument (Albert Gómez 2007; Merriam 1998). More specifically, this article takes the form of a case study (Gillham 2000; Silverman 2005), which can be defined in part as exploratory, since it presents propositions for further inquiry, and in part as descriptive, since a pattern-matching process has been used to analyse data. To be precise, the present study goes beyond a single case study since it involves six case studies of six uni-versity lecturers in three universities. The case studies were chosen by means of criterion sampling (Duff 2008) based on two criteria: (1) a mixed university experience (long-term or short-term) of ICLHE at the tertiary level; (2) different lecturer profiles (age and length of teaching experience).

The observations were non-obtrusive and semi-structured following a template to take field notes (Dörnyei 2003; Mackey & Gass 2005; Marshall & Rossman 1994). The recordings, to which the lecturers consented, were made using two normal MP3 recorders and then transcribed according to

Gail Jefferson's system, which was chosen as it was found easy to read and interpret (see Appendix for the transcription conventions).

The academic context of the lectures

The first institution analysed was founded in Northern Italy in the mid-14th century and is thus one of the oldest state universities in Italy. In 2009, one of the scientific faculties created an entire degree programme and a master's programme solely in English. The university has a strong tradition in the teaching of science and collaborates with the international scientific community in fields such as stamina cells, nanotechnology, material physics, microelectronics and applied biology. It is a member of the Coimbra Group, a network of historic European universities.

The second university is also located in Northern Italy and was founded in the mid-19th century. It is a state scientific-technological university that academically prepares engineers, architects and industrial designers, and participates in numerous research and training projects together with the most prestigious universities in Europe, while continuing to reach out to other countries: from North America to Southeast Asia and Eastern Europe. It has always had an interest in internationalisation, offering numerous exchange programmes and joint degrees in English.

The third university was founded in the 1980s and is based in Central Italy. As far back as the Middle Ages this area had study associations similar to universities; thus there is a tradition with very old roots. This state university has many faculties, both scientific and liberal arts, as well as an entire master's programme in English in the agricultural faculty, which is one of the most important in Italy.

Participants

The lecturers were either directly contacted following an internet search or reached by their Director of Studies following a conversation with the researcher. Lecturers were asked whether they would agree to be observed and audio recorded for at least three hours of lecturing.

Even though the study does not focus on students, some information on the student profiles and target students is included so as to better contextualise the lectures. There were 70 students for the Physics lectures, 8 of whom were non-native-Italian speakers; 80 for Methods in Biochemistry (10 non-native); 80 for Architectural Planning (20 non-native); 20 for Ground Resonance (2 non-native); and finally, 5 for Agroecology and Food Quality (1 non-native). The courses were open to all students regardless of their level of English, thus providing a mix of students at all skill levels.

As far as the profile of the lecturers is concerned, Table 1 provides a summary of their backgrounds and subjects taught. The lecturers' names have been withheld to guarantee anonymity. All lecturers were native Italians and male.

The disparity in the number of words indicates that the lecturers used the three hours of recording in varied ways. For instance, in some cases the lecturers applied the so-called academic 'quarter of an hour', which is a custom in some European countries resulting in the university lecture to start fifteen minutes after the set hour for the class. There was also no uniformity in the use of a break midway through the lectures, with some professors using it and some not. At times the lecturers went on past the end of the lecture, in which case the lecture was longer than three hours. The Agroecology lecture represented a particular case, with the first two hours taken up with a lecture while the final hour was an interview with a local farmer with questions from the lecturer. It should be emphasized that a comparison between the number of minutes of the recording and the number of words was not calculated since, at times, the students asked questions which were not transcribed, as this was beyond the scope of the study.

Table 1. Synoptic table showing the characteristics of the sample

University	Lecturer	Years of teaching	Study programme	Topic	Length (words)	Length (time)	No of students
1	1A	41	Bachelor in Medicine and Surgery	Physics	16,973	3h2'14"	70
1	1B	36	Master in Biology and Genetics	Methods in Biochemistry	22,411	3h3'43"	80
2	2A	25	Bachelor in Architecture and Society	Architectural Planning	28,880	3h12'01"	80
2	2B	14	Master in Rotary Wing Technologies	Ground Resonance	12,400	2h00'44"	20
3	3A	44	Master in Agroecology and Organic Farming	Agroecology	10,140	2h20'19"	5
3	3B	26	Master in Agroecology and Organic Farming	Food Quality	13,561	2h32'02"	5

Results

The present and subsequent sections will comment on several extracts that have been included in specific categories so as to make them easier to interpret. For brevity's sake, only the most significant examples are provided, with the particularly significant parts given in bold print and, where possible, examples were taken evenly from all the lecturers observed. As the six lectures analysed are very specific in terms of their scientific content, a brief contextualisation of the topics covered together with a comment on their meaning is given for each extract.

In light of the description in the literature review (see Figure 1), the occurrences of FonF in the extracts have been categorized as:

1. lexical pre-emptive FonF (Ellis 2001), in which, during a discourse focused on meaning, a lexical element is explained or its meaning provided;
2. grammatical pre-emptive FonF (Ellis 2001), in which the lecturer deals with a grammar element during a discourse on meaning;
3. typographical input enhancement (Sharwood Smith 1993; White 1998), that is, moments where the input is in some way made visible to the learners;
4. code-switching, where the teacher translates a lexeme or an expression from one language to another, thereby focusing on the linguistic form.

A numerical calculation of the categories in question has also been undertaken. Overall, the absolute number of occurrences is not very high (N = 76), that is 76 FonF episodes occurred during the lectures. But, even if rather sporadic, they represent attention given to language. It should be noted that each lecturer showed a preference for particular types of FonF: all of them used the pre-emptive FonF, four the grammatical FonF, three code-switching, and two typographical input enhancement.

The data in Table 2 show that the lecturers used mainly lexical pre-emptive FonF and code-switching through translation of terms. The assumption is that this greater focus on lexical forms and lesser focus on grammatical ones could be due to the fear subject-matter lecturers have of

Table 2. Synoptic table of occurrences, in absolute numbers, of the various types of FonFs

	Lexical Pre-emptive FonF	Grammatical Pre-emptive FonF	Typographical Input Enhancement	Code-switching
Occurrences	25	4	12	35

crossing over into an area they do not feel competent in: language teaching. In fact, the lexical clarifications are less explicitly recognisable as language features and less specifically linked to language teaching; thus, lecturers feel freer to use them.

Lexical pre-emptive Focus on Form
This section gives examples from the corpus of lexical pre-emptive FonF (Ellis 2001), wherein, during a discourse focused on meaning, a lexical element is explained or its meaning provided.

In extract (1) lecturer 1A explains the meaning of the technical term *hematocrit*, which is a keyword in the entire discourse that follows. Since this is a technical term, he must explain it so as to allow the students to better remember and refer to this word, which they have probably never seen before, as they are in their first year of the bachelor's programme. Subsequently, to show that the teacher wants students to clearly understand the lexeme, he uses an example to make the input more understandable.

(1) there is (.) **a value called hematocrit (.) its definition is that this is the percentage volume occupied by erythrocytes** (.) you take for example one cubic centimetre you take all the red blood cells in one-one one side (.) well (.) the volume they occupy in percentage is called hematocrit value (3.0)

In extract (2) lecturer 1A starts with a question which the observations show has been understood by the audience as a rhetorical one. The lecturer immediately goes on to explain the collocation *rigid matter* with the paraphrase *infinite binding force*, precisely because he wants to give an explanation that is closely tied to Physics. The reason for this is that the word *rigid* is probably known by the students since it is a Latin cognate, though they may not know its scientific meaning. In this case, the lecturer again proceeds with an example, thereby showing his interest in focusing on the meaning of the term in order to make it understandable to the students.

(2) **what means rigid matter? rigid mean infinite binding force between the parts of the matter** (3.0) the molecules for example (2.0) deformable matter means that the bonding is finite (.) and the bonding has the characteristic to be dependent on the deformation state of material (10) the finite bonding force is (.) called cohesion force

In extracts 3 and 4 below, lecturer 2A provides a pre-emptive FonF, explaining two lexemes (first using a general explanation and then using a more technical one) which he probably assumes the students are not familiar with (*guild* and *steriotomy*).

(3) when you had the stone masons guild (.) **you know what a guild is? (.) the association of stone masons**

(4) **steriotomy means** eh basically **steriotomy is the geometrical size applied to stone cutting**

In extract (5) lecturer 2B tries to explain a very specific term, *damping*, and begins by saying *in the frequency domain*; however, he then realises he has not been clear and reiterates, trying to explain it more adequately.

(5)   elastomeric dampers which behave according to what is termed the-the complex models
       which means that damping is something in the complex eh eh in-in the frequency
       domain the **damping is a force that is eh ninety degrees ninety degrees delay with
       respect to the motion**

In extract (6) lecturer 3A uses a type of pre-emptive FonF through the use of keywords. It is the beginning of the lecture and so he uses the first keyword as a starting point by saying there are three lexemes the students must remember (the first is *fast*). As soon as he introduces the word he immediately checks that they have understood its meaning by asking a question (*what fast means?*) and through a contextualised explanation (*means that*). The students almost certainly already know the common meaning of the word, but it takes on a more precise meaning (*30 minutes*) in the context of the specific topic of the lecture.

(6)   as you can see **there are three or four** uh (.) **keywords** (.) the first word is fast (.) **what
       fast means?** (.) **means that we have to pre cool** (.) between 30 minutes and one hour
       (.) fast equals efficiency (.) **what means immediately** (.) **after harvest?** (.) **immediately
       means six hours five hours?** (.)

In the following extract (7) the same lecturer chooses a general service word used in a technical sense, *trim*, and paraphrases it to make sure the students are clear about its meaning (*taking away the leaves that are outside*). From the observations it is clear the students do not know its meaning, and so he provides an explanation. In this case his anticipation seems to be a pre-emptive FonF.

(7)   can **trim** (.) **do you know what I mean when I say trim?** (.) **let's say fennel is like that
       I trim** (.) **taking away the leaves that are outside** (.) so what happens? I can use with
       artichokes and then I take I trim I take away the outside leaves (.) I can use with broccoli
       (.) I can use with (.) let's say (.) onions (.) because after the ice pre cooling I can trim ( )
       in this way (.)

Extract (8) is presented because it does not illustrate a true FonF but a circumvented one. Lecturer 3A is unsure whether or not the students know the term *foam* and so he asks for it explicitly (*do you know what I mean by foam*). The observations reveal that the students nodded to let him know they needed no further explanations. In this sense we go back to what Ellis (2008) said about a type of teacher intuition that tells them if it is necessary to turn to form. In this case the lecturer tests the students first to be sure he does not have to turn to FonF.

(8)   so what I suggest to use the proper harvest containers (.) first (.) put some foam on the
       bottom of the (.) container second use foam **do you know what I mean by foam ok?** (.)
       ok

In extract (9) lecturer 3B is introducing the topic of the lecture: Agroecology teaching. Right at the beginning he gets the students to focus on the keyword: *if you take the word evolution*, whose meaning he explains later (*evolution means*). In these few words he has already summed up the entire content of the lecture, which will be a historical *excursus* on Agroecology teaching. As mentioned above, the use of keywords, in particular focusing the students' attention on these, is an example of pre-emptive FonF. As this extract shows, these words are very useful at the beginning or end of the lecture because they offer a summary of the topics.

(9)   **to focus an emphasis on some words** just because the meaning of these words is important for the aim of understanding agro-agroecology teaching dimension in Europe in the context of Europe (.) so the subject is (.) agroecology teaching the subject (.) but you have to- to see this subject (.) with some other (.) contextual eh specialities and particularities and **if you take the word evolution** (.) **evolution means historical development** (2.0) so we see evolution as historical development (.)

Grammatical pre-emptive Focus on Form

This section presents examples of grammatical pre-emptive FonF, in which the lecturer deals with a grammar element while focusing mainly on meaning. There are very few examples of grammatical pre-emptive FonF in the corpus analysed and all of them refer to the use of modals. As these instances occur only when the distinction in modality is relevant to disciplinary concepts or facts, they confirm the above-mentioned assumptions that the content lecturers tend not to deal explicitly with linguistic aspects. On a speculative note, it could be interpreted that grammatical clarifications were seen as too obvious an instance of linguistic focus, and thus the lecturers did not feel competent to deal with them.

In extract (10) one of the lecturers, 1B, actually suggests a strictly linguistic-grammatical change, asking the students to replace *can* with *must*, arguing that *if you do not attach the ligand to the matrix you lose everything.* He then says he does not understand how the writers of the text could have ever used the term *can* when the choice is obligatory. In this way he indirectly and implicitly brings to the students' attention the different uses of *can* and *must* which, among other things, as modal verbs are an integral part of scientific English.

(10) I was telling you that the (.) **verb can should be replaced by another one that is** (.) **must** (.) because if you do not attach your ligand to the matrix through a covalent bond (.) you may lose everything (.) **so I don't understand why they have use this verb can** (.) ok? (2.0)

In extract (11) lecturer 2B corrects himself, emphasising the difference between *may* and *do suffer*. It is noteworthy that during the observation he also indicates meaning (*may* and *do suffer*) through the intonation he gives to the two modals.

(11) we have just found out from a purely mechanical mass and and and spring analysis that an articulated and soft in plane rotor may suffer from instability in the range from (.) zero to 100% rpm (.) **I say may-they actually they do suffer from this problem there is no way you can avoid it**

In the final extract (12) lecturer 3A implicitly asks a grammar question, indicating to the students that he is using the word *must* and not *may* or *maybe*, since companies exporting a product must provide a certificate.

(12) if from Italy I want to export my commodities harvest during the summer time (.) and I want to export to northern European countries (.) like France Switzerland Norway (.) Germany and so on (.) you must (.) add (.) to your commodity (.) the certificate (.) **you must** (.) **not you can or you may or maybe** (.) **you must add** a certificate that says that this lettuce or this artichoke or whatever commodity that you harvested during the summertime (.) has been pre cooled (2.0)

Typographical input enhancement

This section provides examples of typographical input enhancement (Sharwood Smith 1993; White 1998); that is, moments where the input is in some way made visible to the learners. In this corpus, input enhancement is carried out only by underlining the key terms in the handouts.

In extracts (13) and (14) below, lecturer 1B continually refers to the text he uses during the lecture, advising the students to underline certain parts, which is clearly a case of focusing on the language, or at least on students' learning strategies. What is more, the teacher immediately makes a linguistic clarification by indicating a keyword (*salt*). At the university level, lexical pre-emptive FonF of keywords embodies very well the needs of a student who is following a course in English, since the keywords play a pivotal role at the level of both meaning and form. In fact, such a strategy focuses attention on lexis through keywords, which perfectly combines form (the lexeme in the foreign language) and content (the meaning of the lexeme).

(13) so (.) let me say that (.) the **first keyword today is salt** so (.) I would like **to** (.) **underline** what is the content of the second sentence of the brochure (.) in which you will find the same (.) you will find the-the word salt uh (.) what is common to all is the central role played by the structure forming salts so (.) as you may understand (.) in order to (2.0) have (.) separation of protein based on this kind of chromatography (.) you should use (.) buffers containing salts ok? buffer containing salts

(14) in-in all cases what you want to eh suggest (.) to **underline** uh is why these types of support are strongly hydrophilic carbohydrates (.)

In extract (15) the same lecturer goes as far as to suggest changing the text he is using, telling the students to remove (typographical input enhancement) the word *changing* because the pH should not be changed. In the same way, in extract (16) he suggests removing or placing in parentheses a suggestion from the written text which he does not subscribe to (changing the pH or the polarity is not compulsory unless the competitive ligand does not work). In this way he continues to interact with and change the handout, which he uses as an outline for the lecture.

(15) **I would suggest to change to correct changing the pH** because (.) uh is never-is never suggested to change the pH (.) you should (.) specifically move your protein (.) using a competitive ligand

(16) normally you change the nature of your buffer (.) adding to the buffer itself (.) a competitive ligand (.) uh (.) changing the pH (.) changing the ionic strength (.) changing the polarity (.) uh may be that you can use them only if the use of the competitive li-ligand does not work (.) so **please put them into brackets and if possible cancel** ok?

In extract (17), 2B explains an equation he has put up on the screen. He tells the students that several new mathematical expressions, which the students most likely find hard to understand, have been underlined using the appropriate symbol. The lecturer has probably combined these written and oral aids, along with the underlining, to assist students in understanding and memorising the terms.

(17) so now the coupled equations are (.) **I have only highlighted the new terms** (.) we have a diagonal contribution to the matrix of the equivalent eh damping matrix for all degrees of freedom (.) you see ξ is the equivalent damping of-of the of the blade damper and CX and CY are the equivalent damping of the two airframe modes (.)

Code-switching

In this section there are examples of code-switching (alternation of L1–L2), understood as moments of pre-emptive FonF; that is, moments when attention is paid to explaining by translating lexis (Coonan 2007; Laufer & Girsai 2008).

In extract (18) lecturer 1A introduces a new topic (*gas embolism*). He then translates a collocation (*gas embolism*) into Italian and indicates to the students that there are two terms that are very similar but offer different meanings, which he then explains. In this case it is a question of two terms that are easily confused in Italian (*gassosa* and *grassosa*), and thus the translation is useful as a pre-emptive FonF.

> (18)   this is called gas embolism (3.0) in next five minutes I will show you this application to circulation (2.0) but uh as is not an easy application I will repeat it next time (3.0) **what is gas embolism?** (4.0) **uh in Italian** (.) **this is (embolia gassosa)** (.) **be careful to the names** (.) **because (gassosa)** (2.0) **you write** (.) **as this** (2.0) **there is another kind of (embolia)** (.) **which in Italian is called (embolia grassosa)** (5.0) this is very different (.) hm (.) so be careful (4.0) when a bone is uh (.) cracked (.) uh the internal part of uh (.) gas goes to circulation and can give rise to this kind of (embolia) (.) is totally different (2.0)

Lecturer 2A makes a clarification using code-switching in extract (19) to explain, probably to the foreign students, that the expression *la fabbrica del Duomo* (building Milan's cathedral) means something that is never finished, since the construction of the Duomo of Milan went on for many centuries. This clarification is very interesting, since the potential FonF occurs in the opposite sense (from Italian to English) and also involves a cultural explanation.

> (19)   but then in Milano to say la (**fabbrica del duomo**) **the duomo's factory** it means something never ends (.)

In extract (20) lecturer 2A teaches the students that the musical notes in English are ABC. This could easily be part of a normal English lecture where the lecturer explains features of language and culture through contrastive analysis.

> (20)   imagine the same interior shape with just the building (.) if you go here it is the same thing but the way it's related to the to-topography it's different (.) just to say that many times events are related it's like a note (.) you cannot say the note **A B and C in English the notes are letter you say do re mi fa**

Discussion and conclusions

The present study started from an interest in examining the degree of attention paid to language in discourse lectures strongly aimed at meaning, and has sought to understand how present this strategy actually is in ICLHE Italian contexts where lecturers use English as the means of instruction. It uses the Focus on Form (FonF) paradigm to illustrate the extent to which the integration of language and content (encapsulated in the acronym ICLHE) occurs in these settings. Two research questions were posed: (1) concerning the extent to which FonF was present in the science lectures given by native speaking Italian lecturers and (2) regarding the types of FonF that were used.

First, examples of pre-emptive FonF were gathered which allowed some elements of content and language integration to be identified in these lectures. In this sense, this type of lecture can be seen as mainly meaning-focused but with incursions into language focus and thus moving gradually onto ICLHE. As, overall, language is surely seen as secondary in importance to content, we are certainly still a long way away from a balance between language and content objectives. At the same time and since some attention is paid to language, we can consider ICLHE as a more appropriate term than EMI (for a discussion of this difference see Smit & Dafouz, this volume).

Second, it is very difficult to draw a demarcation line between activities centred on meaning and those centred on form. The analysis of the data indicates that there are points in common between these two foci, especially when dealing with an explanation of a technical term which, by definition, is mono-referential, precise and transparent, and when "every term is representative of every concept" (Gotti 1991: 18). Such moments could well embody the concept of integration or, more precisely, that of fusion (Coyle, Hood & Marsh 2010) of the dichotomy between form and content. Thus, technical words can be seen as the meeting point between content and language, since "learning technical words is closely connected with learning the subject" (Nation 2001: 204). In this sense the dichotomy between language and content objectives would disappear in favour of a true integration or fusion, a claim also made by Stohler (2006).

Third, some findings led this study to a theoretical redefinition of the concept of code-switching in classroom discourse. As indicated before, the decision was made to include code-switching in the examples of lecturers' pre-emptive FonF. While Coonan (2007) and Laufer and Girsai (2008) have suggested the inclusion of contrastive analysis and the translation of lexical forms as a means for FonF, the suggestion made here was to expand the definition of pre-emptive FonF by including code-switching as a way of explaining and translating lexis or whole expressions with regards to teacher input. The observations in this study have shown that this strategy is used in situations where there were some non-native Italian speakers, in which case pre-emptive FonF was used to ensure that these students got a good basis in Italian and understood certain cultural concepts. In addition, code-switching was also used in lectures where there was a preponderance of Italian speakers to provide students the lexis in both languages (L1 and L2), especially with regard to both technical and general service terms which learners most likely did not know.

The final issue is of a pedagogical nature and motivated by the truly interesting finding that all the lecturers observed in some way or another paid some attention to the linguistic form and to its teaching, despite being subject-matter lecturers and declaring they were interested in teaching only content (Costa in press; see Airey this volume). This is also indicative of the limited ways in which linguistic forms are actually dealt with and the possibilities for improving the current lecturing style through explicit awareness raising about FonF and its relevance for language learning. All this provides interesting material for future ICLHE methodological training for university lecturers. It is quite difficult to imagine that experienced subject specialists with a high social status (such as Italian university lecturers) will adapt to following ICLHE methodological training or accept English language training (see also Aguilar & Rodríguez 2012). Nonetheless, it is important that they receive some input on how to carry out their lectures through English and on how to deal with language objectives as well. Since it can be difficult for the institutions in question to impose a traditional training course, perhaps training should be rethought of as an exercise in self-awareness, self-discovery, and personal internalisation. In this sense, it is possible to think about providing subject-matter lecturers with evidence of their use of language when a communication problem is somehow sensed, as revealed in this corpus. This could represent the starting point for a type of training focused on reflection, which could provide a new-found role for language lecturers in the ICLHE context. In fact, the language colleague could be a facilitator who brings out the positive aspects and attention to language already present in subject-matter lecturers, so that both groups can work together to further develop these shared assumptions. Thus, methodological training could start with a non-judgmental observation of the lesson by the language academic staff and move on to a series of meetings which present examples of attention to language content that initially lecturers are not aware of. From here the course can be broadened to demonstrate how a focus on language can be expanded in order to fully exploit the potential of ICLHE. The support of the language academic staff may help the content lecturers not to feel so inadequate when focusing on language, thereby favouring progress towards more collaboration across the academic sectors.

Despite being focused on the Italian context, the study has more general applicability and it also comes at a particularly important time for ICLHE during a second wave of ICLHE programmes launched by universities given their increasing interest in internationalisation. In other words, this is the moment for increased research on the topic and for advocating changes where needed.

Acknowledgements

I would like to thank Professor Jim Coleman and Professor Maria Pavesi for their invaluable suggestions for this study.

Notes

1. The two terms, Focus on Form and form-focused instruction (even if the latter, in theory, should also incorporate the former concept), have by now become synonymous, with Focus on Form being the more widely used one. For a summary see Doughty & Williams (1998).

2. Hereafter, the term code-switching is used as a synonym for translanguaging, even though the latter typically refers to the use of two languages according to the task that is involved. García (2009: 47) also refers to it as "languaging bilingually within the same domain".

References

Aguilar, M. & Rodríguez, R. 2012. Lecturer and student perceptions on CLIL at a Spanish university. *International Journal of Bilingual Education and Bilingualism* 15(2): 183–197.

Albert Gómez, M.J. 2007. *La investigación educativa: claves teóricas*. Madrid: Mc-Graw-Hill.

Baker, C. 2006. *Foundations of Bilingual Education and Bilingualism* (4th ed.). Bristol: Multilingual Matters.

Brinton, D., Snow, M. & Wesche, M. 1989. *Content-Based Second Language Instruction*. New York: Newbury House.

Butzkamm, W. 1998. Codeswitching in a bilingual history lesson: The mother tongue as a conversational lubricant. *International Journal of Bilingual Education and Bilingualism* 1(2): 81–99.

Camilleri, A. 1995. *Bilingualism in Education: the Maltese Experience*. Tübingen: Julius Groos.

Coleman, J.A. 2006. English-medium teaching in European higher education. *Language Teaching* 39(1): 1–14.

Cook, V. 2001. Using the first language in the classroom. *The Canadian Modern Languages Review/La révue canadienne des langues vivantes* 57(3): 402–423.

Coonan, C.M. 2007. Insider views of the CLIL class through teacher self-observation-introspection. *International Journal of Bilingual Education and Bilingualism* 10(5): 625–646.

Costa, F. in press. Content lecturers' views of teaching through English in an ICLHE context. In *CLIL: Research, Policy and Practice*, S. Breidbach & B. Viebrock (eds). Frankfurt: Peter Lang.

Costa, F. & Coleman, J. 2012. A survey of English-medium instruction in Italian higher education. *International Journal of Bilingual Education and Bilingualism* 15(1): 1–17.

Coyle, D., Hood, P. & Marsh, D. 2010. *CLIL Content and Language Integrated Learning*. Cambridge: Cambridge University Press.

Creswell, J.W. 1998. *Qualitative Inquiry and Research Design: Choosing Among Five Traditions*. London: Sage.

Dafouz, E. 2007. On content and language integrated learning in higher education: The case of university lectures. *Revista Española de Lingüística Aplicada*. Volumen Monográfico (Special Issue): 67–82.

Dafouz, E. 2011. English as a medium of instruction in Spanish contexts. In *Content and Foreign Language Integrated Learning*, Y. Ruiz de Zarobe, J. M. Sierra & F. Gallardo del Puerto (eds), 189–209. Bern: Peter Lang.

Dafouz Milne, E. & Núñez Perucha, B. 2010. Metadiscursive devices in university lectures. In *Language Use and Language Learning in CLIL Classrooms*, C. Dalton-Puffer, T. Nikula & U. Smit (eds), 213–231. Amsterdam: John Benjamins.

Dafouz, E., Nuñez, B. & Sancho, C. 2007. Analysing stance in a CLIL university context: Non-native speaker use of personal pronouns and modal verbs. *The International Journal of Bilingual Education and Bilingualism* 10(5): 647–662.

Dafouz, E., Núñez, B., Sancho, C. & Foran, D. 2007. Integrating CLIL at the tertiary level: Teachers' and students' reactions. In *Diverse Contexts-Converging Goals: CLIL in Europe*, D. Marsh & D. Wolff (eds), 91–101. Frankfurt: Peter Lang.

Dalton-Puffer, C. 2007. *Discourse in Content-and-Language-Integrated Learning (CLIL) Classrooms*. Amsterdam: John Benjamins.

Dörnyei, Z. 2003. *Questionnaires in Second Language Research*. Mahwah: Lawrence Erlbaum.

Doughty, J. & Williams, J. 1998. Issues and terminology. In *Focus on Form in Classroom Second Language Acquisition*, C. Doughty & J. Williams (eds), 1–11. Cambridge: Cambridge University Press.

Duff, P. 2008. *Case Study Research in Applied Linguistics*. New York: Routledge.

Ellis, R. 2001. Introduction: Investigating form-focused instruction. *Language Learning* 5: 1–47.

Ellis, R. 2008. *The Study of Second Language Acquisition*. Oxford: Oxford University Press.

Ellis, R.; Basturkmen, H. & Loewen, S. 2001. Preemptive focus on form in the ESL classroom. *TESOL Quarterly* 35(3): 407–432.

Fortanet, I. 2008. Questions for debate in English medium lecturing in Spain. In *Realizing Content and Language Integration in Higher Education*, R. Wilkinson & V. Zegers (eds), 21–31. Maastricht: Universitaire Pers Maastricht.

Fortanet-Gómez, I. 2010. Training CLIL teachers for the university. In *CLIL in Spain: Implementation, Results and Teacher Training*, D. Lasagabaster & Y. Ruiz de Zarobe (eds), 257–276. Newcastle upon Tyne: Cambridge Scholars Publishing.

Gajo, L. 2001. *Immersion, Bilinguisme et Interaction en Classe*. Paris: Didier.

García, O. 2009. *Bilingual Education in the 21st Century*. Malden: Wiley-Blackwell.

Gass, S.M. 1997. *Input, Interaction, and the Second Language Learner*. Mahwah: Lawrence Erlbaum.

Gass, S.M. & Madden, C.G. 1985. *Input in Second Language Acquisition*. Cambridge, MA: Newbury House.

Gillham, B. 2000. *Case Study Research Methods*. London: Continuum.

Gotti, M. 1991. *I linguaggi Specialistici. Caratteristiche Linguistiche e Criteri Pragmatici*. Firenze: La Nuova Italia.

Greere, A. & Räsänen, A. 2008. *LANQUA. A QualityTool for Languages*, ⟨http://www.lanqua.eu/sites/default/files/LanQua_frame_of_reference.pdf⟩ (16 June 2012).

Housen, A. & Pierrard, M. 2005. Investigating instructed second language acquisition. In *Investigations in Instructed Second Language Acquisition*, A. Housen & M. Pierrard (eds), 1–27. Berlin: De Gruyter.

Krashen, S.D. 1985. *The Input Hypothesis: Issues and Implications*. Lincolnwood: Laredo Publishing.

Laufer, B. & Girsai, N. 2008. Form-focused instruction in second language vocabulary learning: a case for contrastive analysis and translation. *Applied Linguistics* 29(4): 694–716.

Legge Gelmini 240/2010. Norme in materia di organizzazione delle università, di personale accademico e reclutamento, nonche' delega al Governo per incentivare la qualità e l'efficienza del sistema universitario, ⟨http://www.camera.it/parlam/leggi/10240l.htm⟩ (Retrieved 19th September 2012).

Loewen, S. 2011. Focus on form: The ongoing debate. In *The Handbook of Research in Second Language Teaching and Learning*, E. Hinkel (ed), 576–592, New York: Routledge.

Long, M. 1991. Focus on form: a design feature in language teaching methodology. In *Foreign Language Research in Cross-Cultural Perspective*, K. de Bot, R. Ginsberg & C. Kramsch (eds), 39–52, Amsterdam: John Benjamins.

Long, M. 1996. The role of linguistic environment in second language acquisition. In *Handbook of Second Language Acquisition*, W.C. Ritchie & T.K. Bhatia (eds), 413–468. San Diego: Academic Press.

Long, M.H. & Robinson, P. 1998. Focus on form. Theory, research and practice. In *Focus on Form in Classroom Second Language Acquisition*, C. Doughty & J. Williams (eds), 15–41. Cambridge: Cambridge University Press.

Lyster, R. 2007. *Learning and Teaching Languages through Content*. Amsterdam: John Benjamins.

Mackey, A. & Gass, S.M. 2005. *Second Language Research: Methodology and Design*. Mahwah, NJ: Lawrence Erlbaum.

Mariotti, C. 2006. Negotiated interactions and repair. *VIEWS — Vienna English Working Papers* 15(3): 33–39.

Marshall, C. & Rossman, G.B. 1994. *Designing Qualitative Research*. London: Sage.

Merriam, S.B. 1998. *Qualitative Research and Case Study Applications in Education*. San Francisco: Jossey-Bass.

Myers, M.J. 2008. Code-switching in content learning. In *Realizing Content and Language Integration in Higher Education*, R. Wilkinson, & V. Zegers (eds), 43–48. Maastricht: Universitaire Pers Maastricht.

Nation, P. 2001. *Learning Vocabulary in Another Language*. Cambridge: Cambridge University Press.

Pavesi, M. & Zecca, M. 2001. La lingua straniera come lingua veicolare. *Studi Italiani di Linguistica Teorica e Applicata* 30: 31–57.

Pérez-Cañado, M.L. 2012. CLIL research in Europe: Past, present and future. *International Journal of Bilingual Education and Bilingualism* 15(3): 315–341.

Pérez-Vidal, C. 2007. The need for focus on form (FoF) in content and language integrated approaches: An exploratory study. *Revista Española de Lingüística Aplicada*. Volumen Monográfico (Special Issue): 39–54.

Ricci Garotti, F. 2009. Potential and problems of university CLIL. In *CLIL Methodology in University Instruction: Online and in the Classroom. An Emerging Framework*, F. Sisti (ed), 215–222. Perugia: Guerra Edizioni.

Sharwood Smith, M. 1993. Input enhancement in instructed SLA. *Studies in Second Language Acquisition* 15: 165–179.

Seedhouse, P. 1997. Combining meaning and form. *English Language Teaching Journal* 51: 336–344.

Serra, C. 2007. Assessing CLIL at the primary school: A longitudinal study. *International Journal of Bilingual Education and Bilingualism* 10(5): 582–602.

Silverman, D. 2005. *Doing Qualitative Research*. London: Sage.

Stohler, U. 2006. The acquisition of knowledge. *VIEWS - Vienna English Working Papers* 3(6):41–46.

Van Patten, B. 2009. Processing matters in input enhancement. In *Input Matters in SLA*, T. Piske & M. Young-Sholten (eds), 47–61. Bristol: Multilingual Matters.

Veronesi, D. 2009. La lezione accademica in contesto plurilingue: prospettive di analisi tra parlato monologico e interazione plurilocutoria. In *Bi- and Multilingual Universities: European Perspectives and Beyond*, D. Veronesi & C. Nickenig (eds), 205–228. Bozen/Bolzano: Bozen-Bolzano University Press.

Wächter, B. & Maiworm, F. 2008. *English-Taught Programmes in European Higher Education. The Picture in 2007*. Bonn: Lemmens.

White, J. 1998. Getting the learners' attention. In *Focus on Form in Classroom Second Language Acquisition*, Doughty & J. Williams (eds), 85–113. Cambridge: Cambridge University Press.

Wilkinson, R. (ed) 2004. *Integrating Content and Language. Meeting the Challenge of Multilingual Higher Education*, Maastricht: Universitaire Pers Maastricht.

Appendix: Transcription conventions

(taken from ⟨http://wwwstaff.lboro.ac.uk/~ssjap/transcription/transcription.htm⟩)

?   question
(.)   pause
        interruption
( )   unintelligible speech
        [comment]
        (parts in Italian)

Author's affiliation and e-mail address

The Open University, United Kingdom

francesca_costa@hotmail.com

Academics' beliefs about language use and proficiency in Spanish multilingual higher education

Inmaculada Fortanet-Gómez

Today, more and more universities in Spain are starting to design language policies, usually including Spanish and English. At the same time, Spain has a special socio-political context since part of its territory is already bilingual. This paper examines the opinions and attitudes of academics at a bilingual Valencian-Spanish university which is about to implement a multilingual policy adding English as a third language of instruction. Therefore, in order to start planning the implementation of the teacher development programme and complementary communication campaigns that are part of the recently approved policy, it was considered important to determine the beliefs of academics regarding their proficiency in the three languages involved and the ways to teach in them (Borg 2003). A questionnaire was distributed to a stratified sample of the lecturers at Universitat Jaume I in order to find out what lecturers believed to be their competence in the three priority languages and to identify what they regarded as the main pedagogical styles used in their discipline. Additionally, lecturers were asked, by means of a semi-structured discussion, about their attitudes towards multilingual teaching. The results of this study shed some light on teacher training needs regarding language and pedagogy and allow for suggestions as to possible measures in support of implementing multilingual language policies.

Introduction

The use of several languages as the medium of instruction, usually including Spanish and English, is one of the policies under discussion in many universities in Spain. However, Spain cannot be considered a homogeneous state, as it has a special socio-political context, with part of its territory already bilingual. In this paper, I focus on the Valencian Community, a bilingual community with Spanish and Valencian, a variety of Catalan. Universitat Jaume I is one of the five public universities in this autonomous region. Since its beginnings in 1991, it has been a bilingual university. In June 2011 a multilingual language policy[1] which included the introduction of English as a third language of instruction through the integration of content and language was approved. The role of academics for the success of this policy is essential, especially with regard to the effective introduction of English as a third language of instruction following a Content and Language Integrated Learning approach. It is assumed that if lecturers possess a high command of the language of instruction, try to use it in an effective way and feel motivated to teach in that language, students will find the introduction of this new language of instruction natural and will not react against it. Therefore, in order

AILA Review 25 (2012), 48–63. DOI 10.1075/aila.25.04for
ISSN 1461–0213 / E-ISSN 1570–5595 © John Benjamins Publishing Company

to start planning the implementation of the recently approved policy with regard to the teacher training programme and complementary communication campaigns, it was considered important to determine academics' beliefs regarding their proficiency as well as their attitudes towards the three languages involved and the ways to teach in them (Borg 2003). Previous research on the topic was reviewed and used as a basis for the methodological decisions taken in the present study.

Content and language integrated learning

Language policies and stakeholder beliefs

Studies on competence and attitudes towards the several languages used in multilingual contexts have generally focused on university students rather than on lecturers (Hellekjaer 2004; Lasagabaster & Huguet 2007). However, the conclusions of these studies are often related to proposals regarding the role of lecturers or general institutional policies. As an example, a study on students' competence and attitudes in a Norwegian university (Hellekjaer 2004) concludes that beginner students are not prepared for English-medium instruction and suggests not only requiring a higher command of the English language by students, but also that lecturers who are willing and prepared should adjust teaching to the proficiency level of students and sort out language and learning difficulties. Unfortunately, this kind of suggestion does not often find fertile soil to grow among today's university academic staff, especially when it is content lecturers who have to integrate content and language instruction, as evidenced by the comments provided by the lecturers at Universitat Jaume I.

Another example of research focusing on students is the volume edited by Lasagabaster and Huguet (2007), which collects the reported language competence and attitudes of students who will eventually become language teachers in 9 bilingual regions in Europe, 4 of them in Spain. The results show relevant differences between regions. In the case of the Valencian Community, the study was carried out at Universitat Jaume I (Safont 2007) and shows how students believe in the superiority of their competence in Spanish and also report a very positive attitude towards this language. There seems to be a clear relationship between reported competence and attitudes towards this language. In their answers, students also believe they have a good competence in Valencian. However, their reported knowledge in English seems to be much lower. Valencian is known well or very well by 75% of students and just 6% report to have no knowledge of this language. In contrast, only 2% affirm to be very good and 36% to be good at English. Half of the students seem to have positive attitudes and 40% neutral attitudes towards Valencian, while 30% show positive and 63% neutral attitudes towards English. The study uncovers a correlation between more positive attitudes towards Valencian by students who come from smaller towns and who have followed a language programme in pre-university education with Valencian as mother tongue. More positive attitudes towards English are associated with having visited a foreign country. These results are interesting not only because they show the competence and attitudes of students at Universitat Jaume I, but also because the individuals in this research may be the teachers of future generations of university students.

On the other hand, in some universities, the requirements stemming from new policies for the incorporation of English as a second or third language of instruction have had various consequences on lecturers, including negative reactions. At the University of Delft (Klaassen 2008) all new personnel need to meet linguistic requirements in English and the entire scientific staff must take tests in this language if they cannot provide any certificate. At Delft, lecturers are required to follow courses to improve their language proficiency to the level of C1, as well as courses on pedagogical skills for English-medium instruction, since it was found that many lecturers were not aware of the complexity of the pedagogical situation when a change of language took place in the classrooms. This type of requirements have given rise to paradoxes: nobody questions the need to introduce English as a language of instruction, but there seems to be a "widespread unwillingness of many teachers to participate in multilingual programmes", as reported by some researchers in a Spanish university where this type of policy has also been implemented (Doiz, Lasagabaster & Sierra 2011:353). Lecturers' main justifications are that they do not understand or share the ways to implement the multilingual language policies, or their perception that teaching in a foreign language requires extra effort and time, something they are not willing to invest.

One of the main general arguments against the introduction of English as a language of instruction has been the possibility of domain loss when only the foreign language is used in certain contexts, such as university education. In Sweden, for instance, Airey (2004) reports on growing scepticism amongst some political parties, but also some lecturers and the population at large, about the spread of English, since it is seen as leading to a situation of diglossia (division in the function and status of languages) in the long term (see also Airey, this volume). Moreover, research on language use in courses taught in English has unveiled that, although most core communicative situations take place in that language (lectures, lab work, examinations and dissertations, e-learning activities), students frequently switch to their mother tongue in non-core activities (social interaction, group work) (Ljosland 2010). A measure taken by some universities to balance the influence of English has been to limit the number of courses taught in this language (cf. Unterberger, this volume) and to introduce mother tongue communication skills courses for students in order to enhance and improve the use of their L1 in academic contexts. Along the same lines, in bilingual areas such as the Basque Country in Spain, lecturers support the idea of introducing classes in English once the demand for compulsory classes in the official languages (Spanish and Basque) has been satisfied, in order to avoid linguistic conflict and the consideration of English as an 'invader' (Doiz, Lasagabaster & Sierra 2011).

Other measures have been taken by universities to avoid negative reactions by lecturers to English-medium instruction, such as introducing pedagogical changes. At the University of Maastricht (the Netherlands), English-medium instruction was carried out in a small scale, interactive and student-centred context, using a problem-based pedagogy (Leeuwen 2003). In the Peninsula Technikon in Cape Town (South Africa), the role of the language lecturers was redefined in order to collaborate with content lecturers with the aim of teaching the disciplinary discourse explicitly. This collaboration led also to the sharing of pedagogical strategies in content and language disciplines, and to a debate about the convenience of combining these strategies in content and language integrated learning (Jacobs 2007).

Content and language integrated learning in Spain

Content and language integrated learning (CLIL) has received much attention in Spain in recent years, as proven by the number of volumes and articles published on this topic (Lasagabaster & Huguet 2007; Cenoz 2009; Dafouz & Guerrini 2009; Lasagabaster & Ruiz de Zarobe 2010; Lorenzo et al. 2011; among others). However, most of these publications have mainly focused on primary and secondary education; CLIL research is still in its first stages in higher education. At tertiary level, as well as in primary and secondary education, CLIL is understood as "a dual-focused approach in which an additional language is used for the learning and teaching of both content and language" (Maljers, Marsh & Wolff 2007:8; for a more detailed discussion on CLIL and related terms see Smit & Dafouz, this volume).

As Lasagabaster and Ruiz de Zarobe (2010) explain in the introduction to their volume, one cannot understand the development of CLIL in Spain without knowing its socio-political context. The Spanish state consists of 17 autonomous regions, 5 of them bilingual with Spanish and their own autochthonous language: the Balearic Islands, the Basque Country, Catalonia, Galicia and the

Valencian Community. The autonomous communities' governments regulate the adaptation of the state educational legislation to their territories. In bilingual communities, co-official regional languages have been mandatory at non-university levels since the 1980s. While each community has followed a different way to implement this obligation, the underlying model followed in all cases was immersion education. This means that attention has been exclusively paid to learning the content through the language, without assessing language learning. The objective was the 'normalisation' in the use of the local language in school settings, after a historical period when it had been banned in all public contexts.[2]

In some Spanish regions, CLIL has been introduced in primary and secondary education as a way to improve the level of foreign languages of their students, especially English. In bilingual communities, CLIL has been used to introduce a third and sometimes a fourth language of instruction and to open a debate about the possibility of changing the model to introduce the second language (which can be the autochthonous language or the state language) from immersion to CLIL. This would mean placing both content and language at the same level and assessing the learning process of both. Multilingual education including three or more languages can be taken as a problem by some teachers and even by some parents and pupils, but in fact it is an advantage since previous research has proved that bilinguals often find it easier to learn and work in third and fourth languages (Baker 2006).

In this paper I will focus on the situation in the Valencian Community, where Valencian, a variety of Catalan, is compulsory for primary and secondary school pupils, not only as a subject but also as a language of instruction in some of their school subjects. There are two main tracks towards multilingual education in this community, depending on whether students start school in Spanish or Valencian. The first language is the main medium of instruction and the second language is introduced progressively. The autonomous government establishes the subjects to be taught in each language in these tracks. However, there are no explicit linguistic objectives in content subjects. It is assumed the language is learned by contact, following the immersion model.

In the Valencian Community, CLIL has only been introduced by means of pilot projects in some public primary and secondary schools, with English as a third language of instruction in some subjects. Alternatively, some schools have opted for specific projects developed by teams of language and content teachers (Ruiz Garrido & Saorin Iborra 2009). At this moment, a new decree about plurilingualism including Spanish, Valencian and English is being discussed by the regional government in order to introduce English as a third language of instruction in primary and secondary education in the next years.

A new decree about plurilingualism including Spanish, Valencian and English has just been approved by the regional government in order to introduce English as a third language of instruction in pre-university education in the next years. In the Valencian Community, the situation is presently such that Spanish is the predominant language of instruction, maybe due to the fact that Spanish is the language of most published teaching materials and also the language in which most lecturers studied themselves. The resulting dearth of courses taught in Valencian, however, is deplorable, firstly, because it breaks the continuum of bilingual education at the moment when students start learning the academic and professional discourse they will have to use in their future professional career (Aparici & Castelló 2011). Secondly, the rare use of Valencian seems to be contrary to the responsibility universities took over after the end of the dictatorship, of preserving and promoting the use of the local languages. Some universities such as Universitat Jaume I would like to change their present practices and protect, enhance and promote further the local language in the future.

In recent years, English has been embraced by Spanish academics as the international language of academia. It is perceived as a language needed by students for their success at university as well as for their future careers (Cenoz 2009; Coleman 2006). While there is general agreement on the importance of this language, its implementation as a language of instruction does not seem to be so evident. The reasons may be the low relevance English has had up to now in pre-university studies, which has led to a low command of this language by students entering the university. In addition, some lecturers may also have low proficiency levels in this language and are thus reluctant to use it in the classroom. The results of the present study will unveil whether this is the case at Universitat Jaume I.

Universitat Jaume I: Context and policies

Universitat Jaume I is one of the five public universities in the Valencian Community. It is located in Castelló, a province in the north of this Spanish autonomous region, which is next to Catalonia. The university has about 14,000 students, of which almost 13,000 are undergraduates, and around 1,300 lecturers. According to its Statutes, Valencian and Spanish are co-official languages,[3] and Valencian has received special support since the foundation of the university in 1991. The knowledge of this language has been especially appreciated and valued for the recruitment of staff; there have been complementary courses of Valencian, and teaching in Valencian has been encouraged. Nowadays almost all internal administrative work is carried out in Valencian and lecturers can choose between Spanish and Valencian as the language of instruction of the courses they teach. Even so, only about 20% of the teaching hours are taught in Valencian, and there is a great imbalance between some degree programmes where teaching in Valencian amounts to over 60% of the time, and others where only Spanish is used as the language of instruction. The percentage of tuition in Valencian at Universitat Jaume I is the highest in the universities in the Valencian Community (Aparici & Castelló 2011). However, following the model of primary and secondary education, there are no linguistic objectives in courses taught in Valencian or Spanish (notice that either of them can be first or second languages depending on students' mother tongue).

Universitat Jaume I has also granted a special support to the English language (in comparison to other Spanish universities), since almost all degree programmes have included a module on English for Specific Purposes (ESP). Some years ago, when the universities were summoned to change the degree curricula, due to the Bologna harmonization process, Universitat Jaume I established that 5% of the credits in the new curricula should be taught in English.[4] This created a new situation. Before, it was the language lecturers who had to find out the needs of ESP in each degree curriculum in order to introduce suitable content in their subjects. Now, it is the English language that has to be introduced in the content disciplines.

Bearing this context in mind, a new multilingual language policy was approved for this university in June 2011, which aims to increase and improve the quality of teaching in Valencian and in English by means of content and language integrated learning. Through the many meetings held, it was observed that one of the main factors for the success of such a policy is the lecturers' proficiency in the languages and their beliefs about multilingual education and its implications.

In the following sections, I will describe how the study was designed in order to find out what teachers know and believe about languages (Borg 2003), their pedagogical styles in their disciplines and the introduction of English as a third language of instruction.

Method

Participants

In order to reach the objective described, I distributed questionnaires to a sample of 78 content lecturers (out of a population of 1,286; NC = 95%, E = 3%)[5] and 11 language lecturers (out of 50).[6] The software used to create and distribute the questionnaire was SurveyMonkey.[7] The 78 content lecturers in the sample were selected randomly from the whole university. They were contacted by email and asked to answer the online questionnaire. If, after several weeks, one of them did not answer, another lecturer was contacted with the same request. It was not possible to make a balanced distribution among faculties, since some lecturers do not teach the same subjects every year and many of them belong to the staff of one department but teach in a different one. Another problem is that many lecturers teach in more than one faculty. This led to a quantitative increase in responses given by the 78 lecturers included in the sample: when distributing them according to the faculties where they teach, their input yielded 93 answers. The distribution was the following: 32 (41%) taught at the Faculty of Technology and Experimental Sciences (TES), 22 (28.2%) at the Law and Economics Faculty (LE), and 39 (50%) at the Humanities and Social Sciences Faculty (HSS). This sample will allow me to make some comparisons between the answers of the lecturers in the three faculties.

Data sources and data collection procedures
The first set of questions included in the questionnaire distributed concerned the informants' self-reported language competence. It was decided that, instead of asking directly about academics' perceived level, it would be more accurate to enquire about tasks relevant to the everyday work of content teachers associated to the four skills: writing, reading comprehension, speaking and listening comprehension. Lecturers are required to present papers at conferences, participate in work meetings, attend lectures, write and publish research articles, read literature in their field and naturally, teach. In Valencian universities it is common that lecturers carry out these tasks using Spanish, Valencian and English. All of these tasks require proficiency in the working languages and it was expected that a number of content lecturers would report not to be able to do these tasks in Valencian and English.

The second group of questions asked about disciplinary differences between content and language teaching practices. The two groups of lecturers — content and language — were asked separately about the pedagogical strategies they use in their classes. By pedagogical strategies I understand modes or teaching styles, which correspond to the different ways in which the content is conveyed in classroom talk. The relevant parameters are interactive/non-interactive and dialogic/authoritative (Morton 2012) as well as participants involved (students only, students and teacher and teacher only). Following this taxonomy, there are four pedagogical strategies or modes which combine these ways to convey classroom talk and which are present in all or almost all disciplines:

a. lecturing: authoritative, non-interactive and teacher only
b. class discussion: dialogic, interactive and includes students and teacher
c. student presentation: non-interactive, dialogic and students only
d. group work: interactive, dialogic and students only

The aim of this group of questions was to see if there are significant differences in the several faculties and between content and language subjects regarding these pedagogical strategies, since the lack of collaboration in the introduction of some of these strategies may result in a hindrance for the introduction of content and language integrated learning.

The third group of questions asked about the content lecturers' beliefs on multilingual education and the introduction of English as a third language of instruction. Following Borg (2003: 370), I understand beliefs as "propositions individuals consider to be true and which are often tacit, have a strong evaluative and affective component, provide a basis for action and are resistant to change". The opinions and beliefs of the lecturers at Universitat Jaume I were considered to be essential for determining whether they are ready to admit changes in their teaching activities or not and what could be done to encourage these changes.

The questionnaire data were complemented with a semi-structured discussion of a focus group of 15 content lecturers participating in a teacher training course. This discussion, which took place during a session of this course, was based on questions aimed to elicit the focus group's attitudes towards the trilingual language policy at the university and the main problems it might trigger as well as special pedagogical needs it might imply.

Results and Discussion

On lecturers' language proficiency

The first objective of this research regarded the self-reported aptitude or competence of lecturers in the three languages of the multilingual language policy: Spanish, Valencian and English. Table 1 summarizes the results obtained.

Table 1. Perceived level of language proficiency by lecturers regarding academic activities

How many languages do you know well enough	Spanish	Valencian	English
to present a paper at a conference?	100.0%	73.1%	76.9%
to participate in a work meeting?	100.0%	88.9%	59.3%
to teach?	100.0%	70.4%	51.9%
to follow a lecture at a conference?	100.0%	85.2%	85.2%
to write a research article?	100.0%	63.0%	70.4%
to read literature in your field?	100.0%	81.5%	88.9%

Spanish is the predominant language in all academic activities. If this were a balanced bilingual society in Valencian and Spanish, the results for the two languages should have been similar. However, it has to be borne in mind that bilingual education has only been present in schools and universities for the last 30 years and very few of the respondents had the opportunity to learn Valencian at school. Except for the case of Spanish, there are many differences in the abilities lecturers report to have in the languages they know. Near 90% can use Valencian in a work meeting, but the percentage falls to 63% when the task to be done is to write a research paper. In general, the results unveil the uses lecturers make of the three languages, Spanish, Valencian and English. Spanish is mainly used for all tasks. Valencian is used for work meetings, especially at Universitat Jaume I; however, it is very rarely found as the language of research at conferences or for the publication of research articles. Even so, over 80% of the lecturers can understand the discourse of their field of research in Valencian when reading literature or attending conference lectures. English, on the contrary, is mainly used as the language of research. In general, of all the skills asked about, reading subject-specific literature seems to be the best known, together with listening to academic lectures (two receptive skills) followed by presenting papers in conferences and writing research articles. Teaching seems to be the most difficult task to be carried out in Valencian and in English, as just over 70% report to be able to do it in the former and only about 52% in the latter.

Lecturers' self-reported low command of English for teaching purposes seems to be the most outstanding finding in this group of questions. Up to now, teaching in English has not been a requirement at Universitat Jaume I, neither has it been essential to know this language in order to carry out any local academic activity. Some lecturers report to be fluent in other European languages rather than English due to their contacts with German, French or Italian institutions and to the literature published in these languages in their respective fields of expertise. Those who report to have a good command of English, have usually been engaged in international research and publications as reflected in their self-evaluated language abilities.

Although these self-evaluations seem to indicate that almost half of the lecturers perceived a lack in necessary language proficiency, these figures do not necessarily mean that all of them need further language training. What might be the case is that the lack of experience in teaching in English might have led to relatively low self-confidence in using this language for teaching. An important point to consider here is that academics reported to have a higher command in this language when carrying out research activities and, even though there are relevant differences between research and teaching discourses, some characteristics of research could be related to teaching tasks. For example, a good command in reading literature or writing academic papers can be very useful when preparing classes in English, since these lecturers already know the terminology in their field and can easily prepare good materials in English. Along similar lines, being able to present papers in English at academic conferences can be a basis to start lecturing in that language. One must not forget that the results in this study show academics' beliefs, not necessarily their real capacity to use English while performing various tasks. As there have not been many opportunities to teach in English at Universitat Jaume I or other Spanish universities, these results may reflect low self-esteem rather than a real picture of what lecturers can or cannot do with their command of the English language.

This argument finds support in the results pertaining to Valencian. While almost 90% of the lecturers that took part in this study felt prepared to use this language in work meetings, only 70% claimed knowing this language well enough to use it in the classroom. The reason for this apparent contradiction may be that what lecturers have reported is rather their confidence in conducting activities they have already done in Valencian. By and large, Valencian is considered a language of predominantly informal, face-to-face interaction, and thus those who are fluent in this language and have a good control of the discourse of the discipline (over 80% can read specialised literature), teaching in this language should not represent a particular difficulty.

On disciplinary differences in pedagogical strategies employed
The second group of questions tried to identify disciplinary differences between content and language teaching practices. Two groups of lecturers, content and language lecturers, were asked about the pedagogical strategies they used in their classes. All language lecturers were ESP teachers as there are no Spanish or Valencian language proficiency courses on offer. Table 2 summarizes their answers.

Overall, both groups reported using lecturing as a main instrument in university teaching and whole class discussion about a topic seems to be more widely used in content subjects, while student

Table 2. Pedagogical strategies used by content and language lecturers

Which of the following pedagogical strategies do you use in your classes?	CONTENT		LANGUAGE	
	YES	NO	YES	NO
Lecturing	80.8%	19.2%	80%	20%
Class discussion about a topic	74.1%	25.9%	63.6%	36.4%
Student presentation	77.9%	22.1%	100%	0
Group work	76.7%	24.3%	90%	10%

presentation and group work is much more common in language classes. As argued by Morton (2012), these four pedagogical strategies or teaching styles are different in three ways: authoritarian voice, type of interaction and participants. Lecturing is mostly monologic and the lecturer represents the authoritarian voice. Although the type of discourse is different as it is addressed to a different audience and in a different context, lectures share these two characteristics with conference presentations. Additionally, both lecturing and conference presentations can be prepared in advance and interaction is reduced to a minimum. These common characteristics and the fact that about 75% of the lecturers feel prepared to present papers may persuade them to try lecturing in English or Valencian.

There are two more pedagogical strategies, student presentation and group work, which are already very commonly found in English classes. Student presentation is again monologic and can be prepared in advance by the student. Moreover, students are used to give presentations in English in the language classes, so it would be good to introduce this pedagogical strategy in more content classes. Regarding group work, the main advantage it has is in the production of written assignments or reports by students, since those who have a good knowledge of the language and/or of the content can help less proficient or knowledgeable students. While group work could also be good practice for spoken discourse, it is difficult to control the language that students use in their meetings (Liojsland 2010). Oral skills can be better practised by means of class discussions, which, however, is probably the pedagogical strategy that is the hardest to introduce in content and language integrated learning classes, at least in English. Class discussions are highly interactive and they presuppose that a reasonable number of students participate together with the lecturer. They are also spontaneous, cannot be fully prepared in advance, and they require a high level of oral skills in the language used. Moreover, English teachers report a low use of this strategy in their classes. In order to use class discussion, content and language lecturers should agree in advance that students practise this skill in the language courses so that it can then be introduced in content classes taught in English.

Up to this point, only one of the languages, English, has been dealt with. This is due to the fact that there are no Valencian or Spanish language courses in the degree curricula at Universitat Jaume I and, therefore, the skills used by content lecturers could not be compared with those used by these languages lecturers. The results obtained in a wider study (Fortanet, in press) show that all students reported to know Spanish and about 90% to know Valencian, since almost all students have had all of their pre-university courses taught in one of these languages.[8]

Furthermore, pedagogical strategies were compared by disciplines, which in this study are captured by the three faculties. Table 3 summarizes the results.

Table 3. Pedagogical strategies used by content teachers in the three faculties

Which of the following pedagogical strategies do you use in your classes?	Technology & Science (TES)		Law & Economics (LE)		Humanities & Social Sciences (HSS)	
	YES	NO	YES	NO	YES	NO
Lecturing	81.3%	18.7%	86.4%	13.6%	71.8%	28.2%
Class discussion about a topic	71.9%	28.1%	72.8%	21.2%	73.6%	26.4%
Student presentation	81.3%	18.7%	77.2%	22.8%	74.3%	25.7%
Group work	81.2%	18.8%	66.6%	33.4%	81.5%	18.5%

The findings reveal slight differences between the use of the strategies when comparing disciplines. While lecturing was found to be most frequent in the Faculty of Law and Economics (LE), student presentation was prevalent in the Faculty of Technology and Experimental Sciences (TES) and class discussion seems to be relevant in all three faculties. It is also noteworthy that group work was not so frequently found in the Faculty of Law and Economics (LE). Nevertheless, further research would be necessary to corroborate these results and to find differences also between disciplines taught in the same faculty such as between Law and Economics, or between Psychology and Humanities. In any case and as reported above (see Table 2), in language classes the participation of students by means of presentations and group work seems to be essential, something that does not happen so often in content classes.

These results seem to be in line with Neumann, Parry and Becher's research (2002), according to which there are pedagogical differences between hard and soft, and pure and applied subjects: hard pure subjects try to enhance the students' logical reasoning, and their capacities to apply and test out ideas derived from the theory learned. Knowledge is related to facts and figures and the main aim of students is professional career progression. In contrast, the curricula of soft pure disciplines is built as "spiral in their configuration, returning with increasing levels of subtlety and insight into already familiar areas of content" (Neumann, Parry & Becher 2002: 407). Content is more qualitative and there is a marked interest in developing the critical perspectives of students. Applied hard and soft sciences share the same contrasts, the difference lies in the relevance of knowledge application to the real world. These priorities set by the disciplines seem to lead to differences in teaching: while disciplines in the humanities give more importance to discussion either of the whole class or in groups, those in science and technology favour laboratory experimentation, which often requires working in groups, field trips and presentation of reports. However, there still seems to be a prevalence of lecturing in all disciplines.

In addition to the differences reported by lecturers in the survey, informal conversations with some of them during a teacher training course for the introduction of English as a language of instruction suggest that there may also be different interpretations of what they understand by lecturing, or how a student or group of students are expected to do a presentation. For example, one lecturer in the Computer Science department explained that their students were used to doing oral presentations which mainly consist in applying a theoretical mathematical model. These are short presentations where what is relevant is the numerical development. Conversely, another lecturer in the Law department affirmed that their students' presentations consist in the argumentation towards the application of a certain law to a case, in the form of a case study. This heterogeneity may also affect language and content subjects. Barron (2002) supports that there are relevant differences between the philosophical bases of EAP and science courses: whereas the former are mainly functionalist, the latter are based on the philosophy of realism. As a consequence, EAP tends to apply task-based learning pedagogies and science problem-based learning. Barron (2002) adds two more conceptual differences between EAP and science classes: an epistemological difference in that EAP emphasizes *carrier content*, while science emphasizes *real content*, and an ontological difference as, very often, the content subject, science in that case, is regarded as a higher status discipline than EAP. In the case studied by Barron, these differences led to serious misunderstandings between content and language teachers, and eventually to the failure of a collaborative venture of integrating content and language teaching. Becoming aware of the several ways of 'doing things' in the classroom, as well as of the different points of view held by lecturers in the several disciplines taught in the same degree course can be essential not only for the successful collaboration of content and language lecturers, but also for cross-disciplinary subjects and the coordination of the several disciplines in a certain degree. Creating new spaces for dialogue and negotiation can be a good opportunity for sharing experiences and practices and the only way for possible interdisciplinary collaborations.

On introducing English as a third language of instruction
A final group of questions asked about the content lecturers' opinions on the introduction of English as a third language of instruction. Table 4 summarizes the questions and their answers.

Table 4. Content lecturers' opinions about the introduction of English as a third language of instruction

	YES	NO
Should subjects taught in English have objectives related to the improvement of the students' command of the English language?	72.9%	27.1%
Is specific teacher training necessary to implement multilingual education?	95.9%	4.1%
Do you think it is important that content and language lecturers coordinate their subjects and collaborate in the subjects taught in English?	83.8%	16.2%

By means of the first question, the intention was to find out the content lecturers' attitude towards the introduction of linguistic objectives in their subjects in preparation of implementing an approach such as CLIL in which content and language objectives have the same status. While most content lecturers had never heard about this approach, almost 72% of the respondents answered positively. This shows that only one fourth of the lecturers thought the language of instruction should not have any weight in the content subjects. In other words, and despite the strong tradition of immersion rather than CLIL education in higher education, it seems that only a relatively small group of lecturers regarded the language objectives in their subjects as interfering with what 'is really relevant', that is, content learning; the majority, on the other hand, arguably supported an integrative approach to content and language.

The second question asked about the content lecturers' opinion on the need of a specific programme of teacher training to support multilingual education. There was near unanimous agreement on this proposal, which indicates the use of several languages for teaching is something new for most lecturers and they feel the need to be advised.

The third question referred to the collaboration of language lecturers with content lecturers in order to coordinate the preparation of the subjects taught in English. Although over 80% agreed, the remaining 20% of the lecturers were still reluctant to carry out such collaboration. This might have various reasons. It could be that some content lecturers may object to what they identify as interference of English lecturers in what they teach and the way they do it. Moreover, language lecturers, who belonged to a department in the Human and Social Sciences Faculty, may seem rather detached from what science and engineering or even economics lecturers are doing. Some researchers have described the difficulties lecturers find in collaborating with colleagues in other disciplines (Neumann, Parry & Becher 2002), while others have focused on the positive effects of such collaborations, especially when language and content lecturers are involved (Jacobs 2007; Wright 2007).

Complementary to the quantitative questionnaire, a group of 15 lecturers attending a teacher training course were asked a number of questions in an open discussion about their attitudes towards the three languages and multilingual education at Universitat Jaume I:

1.   Do you think Spanish, English and Valencian should be used as languages of instruction in all undergraduate studies at Universitat Jaume I?
2.   Do you think all three languages should also be used at graduate level?
3.   What can be the main problems to implement trilingual education at Universitat Jaume I?

4.   Is a special pedagogy needed to teach in a second or third language through CLIL?

These questions were more general than those in the questionnaire and were intended to obtain not only the opinions of the group of lecturers, but also those of other colleagues in their departments. In general, lecturers seemed to be in favour of multilingual education with the presence of the three languages in undergraduate studies. On the graduate level, however, there was a tendency to favour only bilingualism in Spanish and English, due to the more international nature of these studies; the presence of Valencian as a language of instruction is not so widely supported. Here a number of answers that denoted certain radicalism should be pointed out. Some lecturers seemed to be in favour of the internationalisation of the university with the introduction of English, but not of Valencian, which is considered by them as a local language that does not contribute to the prestige of the university. This opinion was expressed by one lecturer who found the support of other lecturers coming from the science and engineering departments. On the other hand, some participants, who said they were reporting the opinions of a group of lecturers in their departments (mainly law and humanities), pointed out the ideological implications of introducing English, which is considered a language of power and colonialism that will have a negative influence on the defence and promotion of the local language. Even though these answers seem to come from a minority of lecturers, they could become an important problem for the balanced co-existence of the three languages, Valencian, Spanish, and English. Therefore, it will be essential to pay special attention to the lecturers holding these opinions in an attempt to convince them about the benefits of multilingualism including the three languages.

Moreover, most lecturers in the group seemed to agree that the main problem for multilingual education is the low language competence of lecturers and students, especially with regard to English. In order to avoid this kind of problem with students, some lecturers would only support the idea of introducing tuition in English provided students can choose between parallel groups in the same subject taught in several languages. The low competence of students in the English language had already been reported by Safont (2007) for a smaller number of students at Universitat Jaume I, as explained above. I also checked this finding by distributing a questionnaire to a sample of 771 undergraduate students from the whole university (Fortanet, in press). The results indicate that whereas about 70% of the students reported they can manage in all academic situations with a good level of Valencian, the percentage fell to about 30% when they were asked about their abilities using the English language. What the students reported on knowing the least was writing long essays or reports in Valencian or English, and speaking fluently in the English language. In general, students were much more confident in their receptive skills (listening and reading) in both languages than in their productive skills (writing and speaking). These results indicate a need to improve students' competence, especially in English, and they partly explain the reluctance of over 27% of the content lecturers who answered the questionnaire to include language objectives in content subjects.

Regarding the need for a specific pedagogy for the integration of the three languages with content, most lecturers lacked a clear idea of what this could mean; only two lecturers who explained during the session they had already worked with CLIL in secondary education widely supported the idea. This finding is in line with Klaassen's observations (2008) at the University of Delft, as reported above, regarding lecturers' unawareness of the pedagogic complexity of the CLIL approach. Fortunately, the need to learn about the specific pedagogy to introduce multilingual education seems to be acknowledged by almost all content lecturers (96%), as shown in the results of the questionnaire.

Conclusions

The aim of this paper was to find out about lecturers' self reported language competence, and about their views on a multilingual language policy, focusing on Content and Language Integrated Learning (CLIL) before its implementation in a Spanish bilingual university, Universitat Jaume I. A multilingual language policy had already been approved by the managing bodies of the university. However, it was important to know how much actual support this policy had among lecturers. The investigative approach to ask lecturers directly for their beliefs was chosen because, as argued by Borg (2003), teachers are the central social agents for educational policies to become reality; their beliefs should thus be heard and taken into consideration. The answers to the questionnaires have revealed that most lecturers supported a multilingual language policy for Universitat Jaume I. Having said this, one of the main hindrances for the implementation of multilingual CLIL may be the lecturers' self-reported language competence, which shows some limitations in their knowledge of Valencian and English, especially regarding their productive skills, i.e. writing and speaking. It is noteworthy that teaching in these languages was considered to be the most difficult task. The questionnaires unveil some differences between the pedagogical strategies followed by content and language lecturers, as well as between those used by the lecturers of the three faculties included in the study. Content lecturers in general favour class discussion about a topic, whereas in language courses it is more common to find student presentations and group work. Lecturing seems to be common in both groups, though it would also be interesting to find out the characteristics of these lectures. The comparison between faculties also shows some differences in the pedagogical strategies used. The answers provided by lecturers seem to prove that there are a variety of different pedagogical strategies followed in the several disciplines, and especially by content and English language lecturers.

However, when stating their limited command of English and Valencian to teach in these languages, lecturers might also have been reporting their fears and reluctance to use them in a new academic situation. In my view, it would not be difficult to change lecturers' perception by comparing teaching with other academic tasks they seem to feel more confident with. For example, almost 77% report to be able to present a paper at a conference in English. Though there are differences in the type of discourse, aim and audience, this situation is rather similar to lecturing, since it is authoritative, non-interactive, only the speaker participates and it can be prepared in advance. Regarding Valencian, most lecturers report to be able to speak it fluently in the context of a work meeting (89%), and to be able to read literature in their field (81%), therefore it should not be very difficult for them to transfer their knowledge and ability to the classroom context.

Another point arising from this study is that some pedagogical strategies, such as writing assignments or students' oral presentations, are interpreted differently in several disciplines. Further research on this respect is needed to find out the characteristics of the main pedagogical strategies found in each discipline.

Academics' beliefs on the multilingual language policy implemented at the Universitat Jaume I were considered a central point in this research. Beliefs were elicited by means of a questionnaire and a semi-structured discussion. While, in general, responses revealed a high level of acceptance, at the same time, some lecturers reported on the existence of some critical positions related to language and ideology that will need special attention.

An additional hindrance also addressed by lecturers is the low level of students' competence in Valencian and English. The international origin of many master students recommends the use of Spanish and English as the languages of instruction at this level. Moreover, the need for a stronger command of the English language in undergraduate students suggests it might be advisable not to introduce it as a medium of instruction until the third or fourth year, giving students time for further preparation. The announced introduction of content and language integrated learning in subjects taught in English in primary and secondary education should also be of aid in this case.

On the whole, and as a conclusion to the study, lecturers seem to be doubtful and insecure about certain aspects of the implementation of multilingual education, even though they do acknowledge its importance for the university.

While the study is built on a stratified sample that can be seen as representative of the lecturers of the Faculties of Law and Economics (LE), of Technology and Experimental Sciences (TES) and of Humanities and Social Sciences (HSS), some limitations have to be acknowledged. The comparison between disciplinary fields has only been done taking into account these three faculties at Universitat Jaume I. Each of them includes a variety of degrees that could also show relevant differences in their pedagogical strategies. This could be explored in more detail in further research. Another limitation in this research can be the group of lecturers who held the semi-structured discussion. As these lecturers were attending a training course for the introduction of English-medium teaching, their opinions might have been biased towards a positive attitude on multilingual education, especially regarding English. It would be good to corroborate their answers with those of other groups of lecturers.

As stated at the beginning of this paper, the results of this research should be considered as part of an initial picture of the present situation at Universitat Jaume I. Further studies will be needed to see the evolution in the language competence and beliefs of the university community after some actions have been implemented.

In the light of the results obtained, several recommendations might help to overcome potential problems of implementing the multilingual language policy. In addition to incentives and linguistic requirements for the promotion of multilingual lecturers, I propose an effective communication campaign and a specific training programme. The communication campaign should reach the whole university community and should have a complementary external campaign, addressed to future students and their families and to the society at large. The internal campaign should aim at convincing students, lecturers and administrative staff that multilingualism is not only useful, but also an added value for this university which can contribute to the tolerance of other views, ideologies and cultures, as stated in the already approved multilingual language policy.

The training programme should have pre-service and in-service courses and one of its aims should be to reinforce the competence of lecturers in their command of Valencian and English for academic purposes. In addition to courses provided by other institutions (Official School of Languages, Cambridge ESOL programme, etc.), and the possibility to take accreditation exams at the university, these courses should aim to help lecturers improve their proficiency in English and Valencian, so that they can teach subjects in these languages, thus supporting language policy plans to reach a balance between the three languages of instruction.

As the objective is that students can use the three languages in academic and professional contexts, which cannot be achieved if the linguistic part of the subjects does not receive any attention, the second aim of the teacher training programme should be to provide information about the CLIL approach and the pedagogies associated with it, with courses and seminars in which both content and language lecturers can participate. Similar to the initiative of the Peninsula Technikon in Cape Town (Jacobs 2007), these courses would invite content lecturers to share their experiences regarding the pedagogical strategies they use and encourage them to collaborate with language lecturers in order to combine their pedagogies in the implementation of the content and language integrated learning approach. Such courses are essential in order to guarantee the success of multilingual education through CLIL in which content and language objectives share the same status.

In this paper I have tried to present some research carried out in a bilingual university in Spain, featuring Valencian, the local language, and Spanish, the national language, before the implementation of a multilingual language policy with English as a third language. Some of the features depicted are common to many universities intending to introduce an additional language of instruction like the problems in language competence and the low self-esteem shown by some lecturers facing the challenge of teaching for the first time in another language; or the difficulties in collaborating with other lecturers due to different pedagogical strategies, a fact many teachers are unaware of. Additionally, multilingual universities present a more complex situation and therefore require more reflection, more planning and a closer follow up. One of the specific problems identified in this paper is the competition between the relevant languages, which may pave the way for critical positions favouring some of the languages and/or against some other, All in all, this paper aims to contribute to the Applied Linguistic research concerns raised in this publication (see Smit & Dafouz, this volume), since teacher beliefs, together with classroom discourse and English-medium policy development and implementation, can all provide a global view of the integration of content and language in today's higher education.

Notes

1. *Pluriannual Plan for Multilingualism* ⟨http://www.uji.es/bin/projectes/docs/ppm-a.pdf⟩ (07/05/2012)

2. The use and promotion of local languages were forbidden in Spain during the 40 years of the Franco dictatorship (1939–1978).

3. *Estatuts de la Universitat Jaume I* ⟨http://www.uji.es/bin/uji/norm/estatuts/estf-val.pdf⟩ (14/03/2012).

4. In Spain 1 credit is the equivalent to 8–10 hours of teaching and 15–17 hours of students' individual work. The equivalence of 5% of the credits is about 12 credits, or 120 hours of teaching, in addition to the English subject (6 credits) that almost all bachelor degree programmes include.

5. An expert in statistics recommended the appropriate number of individuals to be included in the sample. This number, 78, gave 95% of normal confidence level and an error of just 3%.

6. The procedure to select the number of language lecturers was different, since the opinions of a more significant number of these lecturers were needed. All 50 lecturers in the Department of English Studies were requested to participate since all of them have at least once taught a subject of English for Specific Purposes in a non-language focused bachelor degree. Finally, 11 (22%) accepted to participate.

7. Survey Monkey ⟨http://www.surveymonkey.com⟩ (17/05/2012)

8. The percentage of foreign undergraduate students at Universitat Jaume I is very low. Only about 3.2% of the students in the sample are exchange students, and about 2% are foreigners (Fortanet, in press).

References

Airey, J. 2004. Can you teach it in English? Aspects of the language choice debate in Swedish Higher Education. In *Integrating Content and Language: Meeting the Challenge of a Multilingual Higher Education*, R. Wilkinson (ed), 97–108 Maastricht: Maastricht University Press.

Aparici, A. & Castelló R. (eds). 2011. *Els Usos Lingüístics a les Universitats Públiques Valencianes.* València: AVL, ⟨http://www.uji.es/bin/serveis/slt/triam/ulupv.pdf⟩ (14 March 2012).

Baker, C. 2006. *Foundations of Bilingual Education and Bilingualism* (4th ed.). Bristol: Multilingual Matters.

Barron, C. 2002. Problem-solving and EAP: themes and issues in a collaborative teaching venture. *English for Specific Purposes* 22: 297–314.

Borg, S. 2003. Teacher cognition in language teaching: A review of research on what language teachers think, know, believe and do. *Language Teaching* 36(2): 81–109.

Cenoz, J. 2009. *Towards Multilingual Education: Basque Educational Research from an International Perspective*. Bristol: Multilingual Matters.

Coleman, J.A. 2006. English-medium teaching in European higher education. *Language Teaching* 39(1): 1–14.

Dafouz, E. & Guerrini, M. (eds). 2009. *CLIL across Educational Levels: Experiences from Primary, Secondary and Tertiary Contexts*. Madrid: Richmond.

Doiz, A.; Lasagabaster, D. & Sierra, J. M. 2011. Internationalisation, multilingualism and English-medium instruction. *World Englishes* 30: 345–359.

Fortanet, I. (in press). *CLIL in higher education: Towards a multilingual language policy*. Bristol: Multilingual Matters.

Hellekjaer, G.O. 2004. Unprepared for English-medium instruction: A critical look at beginner students. In *Integrating Content and Language. Meeting the Challenge of a Multilingual Higher Education*, R. Wilkinson (ed.), 147–161. Maastricht: University of Maastricht Press.

Jacobs, C. 2007. Integrating content and language: Whose job is it anyway?. In *Researching Content and Language Integration in Higher Education*, R. Wilkinson & V. Zegers (eds), 35–47. Nijmegen: Valkhof Pers.

Klaassen, R. 2008. Preparing lecturers of English-medium instruction. In *Realizing Content and Language Integration in Higher Education*, R. Wilkinson & V. Zegers (eds), 32–42. Maastricht: Maastricht University Press, ⟨http://arno.unimaas.nl/show.cgi?fid=12521⟩ (15 March 2012).

Lasagabaster, D. & Huguet, À. (eds). 2007. *Multilingualism in European Bilingual Contexts. Language Use and Attitudes*. Bristol: Multilingual Matters.

Lasagabaster, D. & Ruiz de Zarobe, Y. (eds). 2010. *CLIL in Spain: Implementation, Results and Teacher Training*. Newcastle upon Tyne: Cambridge Scholars Publishing.

Liojsland, R. 2010. Teaching through English: Monolingual policy meets multilingual practice. *Hermes — Journal of Language and Communication Studies* 45: 99–113.

Lorenzo, F.; Moore, P. & Casal, S. 2011. On complexity in bilingual research: The causes, effects, and breadth of content and language integrated learning: A reply to Bruton. *Applied Linguistics* 32(4): 450–455.

Maljers, A.; Marsh, D. & Wolff, D. 2007. *Windows on CLIL, Content and Language Integrated Learning in the European Spotlight*. ECML Graz.

Morton, T. 2012. Classroom talk, conceptual change and teacher reflection in bilingual science teaching. *Teaching and Teacher Education* 28: 101–110.

Neumann, R.; Parry, Sh. & Becher, T. 2002. Teaching and learning in their disciplinary contexts: A conceptual analysis. *Studies in Higher Education* 27(4): 405–417.

Ruiz-Garrido, M.F. & Saorín-Iborra, A.M. (eds). 2009. *Hacia una Educación Plurilingüe: Experiencias Docentes AICLE*. Castellón: Publicacions de la Universitat Jaume I.

Safont, M.P. 2007. Language use and language attitudes in the Valencian community. In *Multilingualism in European Bilingual Contexts. Language Use and Attitudes*, D. Lasagabaster & Á. Huguet (eds), 90–113. Bristol: Multilingual Matters.

Van Leeuwen, C. 2003. Feasibility of policy in university language teaching today. In *Multilingual Approaches in University Education. Challenges and Practices*, C. van Leeuwen & R. Wilkinson (eds), 19–45. Maastricht: University of Maastricht Press.

Wright, J. 2007. Key themes emerging from co-authoring during a content and language integration project. In *Researching Content and Language Integration in Higher Education*, R. Wilkinson & V. Zegers (eds), 82–95. Nijmegen: Valkhof Pers.

Author's affiliation and e-mail address

Universitat Jaume I, Spain

fortanet@ang.uji.es

"I don't teach language"

The linguistic attitudes of physics lecturers in Sweden

John Airey

From a disciplinary discourse perspective, all university courses can be said to involve content and language integrated learning (CLIL) even in monolingual settings. Clearly, however, things become much more complex when two or more languages are involved in teaching and learning. The aim of this paper is to introduce readers to the linguistic situation in Swedish universities, where two languages — English and Swedish — are commonly used in the teaching and learning of a number of disciplines. The paper describes the linguistic landscape of Swedish higher education and presents an illustrative case study from a single discipline (physics) with a hierarchical knowledge structure (Bernstein 1999). Semi-structured interviews were carried out with ten physics lecturers from four Swedish universities. The lecturers were asked about their disciplinary language-learning expectations for their students. These interviews were analysed using qualitative methods inspired by the phenomenographic approach. Six main themes resulting from the analysis are presented and discussed. From a CLIL perspective, one recurring theme is that none of the lecturers saw themselves as teachers of disciplinary Swedish or English. The paper concludes by discussing the generalizability of the findings to other disciplines with similar (hierarchical) knowledge structures.

Introduction

The term content and language integrated learning (CLIL) is generally used to describe the situation where students learn a language other than their L1 at the same time as they learn their subject specialization (for a more detailed discussion of CLIL see Smit & Dafouz, this volume). At university level in Sweden, the CLIL approach has often been deemed untenable since language learning goals are seldom specifically mentioned in course syllabuses. However, it could be argued that from a disciplinary discourse perspective, all university courses involve CLIL *even in monolingual settings* (see Northedge 2002 for a description of the specialist disciplinary language-learning needs of undergraduates). Put simply, the claim made here is that all teachers are language teachers. A relatively uncontroversial version of this claim has been expressed by Lemke (1990), who points out that disciplinary learning critically depends on the ability to interpret and control the specialized language in which the knowledge is construed. At the other end of the spectrum, a more radical version of this claim has been put forward by Wickman and Östman (2002), who insist that learning itself should be seen as a form of discourse change.

Whichever of these commitments one subscribes to, undergraduate learning in a monolingual setting undoubtedly involves some measure of disciplinary language learning — discipline and

AILA Review 25 (2012), 64–79. DOI 10.1075/aila.25.05air
ISSN 1461–0213 / E-ISSN 1570–5595 © John Benjamins Publishing Company

language are inextricably entwined. Clearly then, disciplinary learning can be expected to become much more complex when two or more languages are involved. In the work presented here CLIL is taken to mean the learning of content together with the disciplinary language(s) needed to interpret and use such content effectively.

The aim of this paper is to introduce readers to the linguistic situation in Swedish universities, where two languages — English and Swedish — are commonly used in the teaching and learning of a number of disciplines. The specific focus of the paper is to illustrate lecturers' attitudes to the development of disciplinary language skills in the two languages used in Swedish higher education. The paper describes the linguistic landscape of Swedish higher education and presents an illustrative case study from a single discipline (physics) with a hierarchical knowledge structure (Bernstein 1999). The situation in Swedish undergraduate physics is interesting in this respect since the default situation is often one of course literature in English and lectures in Swedish: however, the enrolment of one overseas exchange student on a course will often change the teaching language to English (Höglin 2002). With this setting in mind, it is interesting to study the linguistic goals that physics lecturers have for their students *in both languages* — what I have termed bilingual disciplinary literacy elsewhere (Airey & Linder 2008; Airey 2009, 2010). How do lecturers see their learning goals when the teaching language of a given course may change from term-to-term?

In what follows, I report on a study in which ten physics lecturers from four Swedish universities were interviewed about their disciplinary language-learning expectations for their students. These interviews are qualitatively analysed resulting in the production of six themes. These findings are then discussed and related to Bernstein's (1999) work on horizontal and hierarchical disciplinary knowledge structures.

Language use in Swedish higher education

The use of English language in higher education is on the increase throughout Europe. This trend is partly the result of an effort to attract new cohorts of overseas students in the wake of the ratification of the Bologna Declaration (Benelux Bologna Secretariat 2007–2010) and partly due to wider themes of international competitiveness and globalization (for more information on these developments see Smit & Dafouz, this volume). A survey of English-taught programmes in European higher education by Wächter and Maiworm (2008) suggests that Sweden is one of the leading countries in this movement towards the increasing use of English.

Whilst many countries in Europe are rushing to expand the use of English in their higher education systems (see Fortanet-Gómez and Unterberger, both this volume) in some respects, the debate in Sweden has already come full circle. Here, the high proportion of English language use in higher education has led to a discussion of the best way to guarantee the continued use of disciplinary Swedish. In the introduction to his recent extensive survey of the language situation in Swedish higher education, Salö (2010) provides a summary of the development of the debate in Sweden. As early as 1992, Teleman warned that an integrated Europe would weaken the use of Swedish in higher education. By 2006 a widespread debate about the possible negative consequences for disciplinary Swedish of the by then already extensive use of English in higher education was in full swing. This debate was played out not only in research circles, but also in vocational publications such as the university lecturers' union newspaper *Universitetsläraren* and the national press. The debate focused on issues of domain loss, diglossia and language protectionism. These worries were weighed against the benefits of English language use for international competitiveness and as the *de facto* language of research. The debate led to a general consensus that *both* English and Swedish were needed in higher education, and the concept of *parallel language use* (Josephson 2005) was adopted. This concept was not without its critics. Airey and Linder (2008) criticized the notion of parallel language use, pointing out that the focus was simply on regulating the teaching languages used in higher education rather than enumerating a set of disciplinary linguistic skills that students, lecturers and researchers need to acquire.

With the idea of parallel language use came the first university language policies. In 2008 the Swedish National Agency for Higher Education (2008) recommended that all Swedish higher education establishments should as soon as practicable produce their own language policy documents. At that point in time only Gothenburg University had such a policy document. Salö (2010) reports that by August of the following year eleven out of a sample of 37 higher education establishments had some sort of language policy document. On the whole these policies have been implemented with the intention of regulating the use of academic English whilst guaranteeing the use of academic Swedish. For example one common requirement is that PhD theses written in English must include a detailed summary in Swedish.

As mentioned earlier, one of the main motivations for the use of English in Swedish higher education is the presence of overseas students given that the presence of one overseas student can force a whole course originally taught in Swedish to be taught in English (Höglin 2002). Recently, however, the number of overseas students in Swedish higher education has decreased dramatically. Traditionally, tuition fees for university education have been fully subsidized by the government, for all students both Swedish and international. This situation changed from autumn term 2011 and Swedish universities are now required to charge fees that completely cover their tuition costs for students from outside the EU and European Free Trade Association. For example, Lund University was forced to charge between 10,000 and 26,000 Euros per academic year depending on the programme. This led to a dramatic decrease in the number of non-European students studying in Sweden, the number falling from 16,600 in autumn 2010 to a mere 1,200 in autumn 2011 (Ekholm & Bennet 2011). Swedish higher education may well have to adapt to this new situation since anecdotal evidence suggests that if overseas students are forced to pay for their tuition then many would rather study in a fully English-speaking environment.

CLIL research in Swedish higher education

In Sweden, the term CLIL is seldom mentioned in higher educational research or curriculum goals. In fact, very few course syllabuses mention language at all, and when they do this is often a simple statement of the teaching language (Airey & Linder 2008). A small number of undergraduate courses are taught in tandem by disciplinary specialists and language specialists notably in Gothenburg and on vocational courses at a number of other universities. However, the notion that one might learn a second or foreign language at the same time as one learns a discipline is the exception rather than the norm. Rather, the situation in the majority of Swedish undergraduate education is one where language competency is seen as a necessary tool for learning rather than an expressed learning outcome. As I explained in the introduction to this paper, I view all disciplinary learning as a form of language learning and thus I view CLIL as an approach that is carried out *de facto* in every course — even when the course is taught exclusively in the students' L1. The focus of this paper, then, will be lecturers' attitudes to the development of disciplinary language skills in the two languages used in Swedish higher education (English and Swedish). The following section describes some of the main research strands in this area.

The majority of Swedish research into language use in higher education has taken the form of surveys. These have examined the extent to which English and Swedish are used and lecturer and student attitudes to the use of English and Swedish (e.g. Bolton & Kuteeva 2012; Falk 2001; Gunnarsson & Öhman 1997; Melander 2005; Pecorari et al. 2011; Salö 2010). These studies have uncovered a linguistic division between the disciplines, with natural sciences, engineering and medicine having the largest proportions of their course literature and some undergraduate teaching in English. At the other end of the spectrum are the humanities where English is used to a much lesser extent. Notable in this line of research is the study by Bolton and Kuteeva (2012) who find differences in disciplinary attitudes to the use of English, with informants in the natural sciences having the most positive attitudes to English and informants in the humanities having the least positive attitudes.

Other work has described the language environments within various disciplines. Working at a Swedish technical university, Björkman (2010) collected a corpus of 70 hours of high-stakes speech events (lectures, and group work) in an English Lingua Franca (ELF) setting. Her analysis of ELF usage finds little breakdown in communication, suggesting that the subjects' non-standard English actually leads to added clarity but with some reduced redundancy. In terms of Swedish, Söderlundh (2010) investigated the effect of the use of English as a language of instruction on the use of Swedish in higher education, finding that despite university courses being nominally taught in English, there is, in fact a large amount of Swedish interaction to be found in such courses.

In terms of student reading, both Karlgren and Hansen (2003) and Söderlundh (2004) suggest that compared with reading in Swedish, reading in English leads to a more surface understanding of content. However, Shaw and McMillion (2008) provide a slightly different picture, suggesting that Swedish students actually comprehend the content of an English biology textbook as well as their British counterparts provided they are given extra time.

Hincks (2010) and Airey (2009, 2010) have compared student speaking rates and content in English and Swedish, finding that students speak more slowly and pause more often in English. This has led to the suggestion that lecturers may also act in a similar way and would therefore need more time to do the same work when moving from teaching in Swedish to teaching in English (Hincks 2010).

Airey and Linder (2007, 2008) found that whilst Swedish students may suggest that they learn equally well from lectures in the local language or English, the same students can point out a number of important differences in their learning when shown video footage of actual lectures in a process of stimulated recall (Calderhead 1981). The differences found relate to difficulty experienced in simultaneously following a lecture and taking notes, and a smaller number of questions asked and answered when lectures were in English. This reduction in the frequency of questions in English-medium instruction was also noted by Björkman (2010).

Finally, Kuteeva and Airey (under review) report a direct relationship between disciplinary knowledge structures (Bernstein 1999) and attitudes to English language use, with disciplines with hierarchical knowledge structures such as the natural sciences being more predisposed to use English than those with horizontal knowledge structures such as the humanities and arts. The study presented in this paper builds on Kuteeva and Airey's findings by examining the language learning expectations of lecturers in one discipline with a hierarchical knowledge structure (physics). The aim is to illustrate the relationship between hierarchical disciplinary knowledge structures and language. A short summary of Bernstein's ideas about disciplinary knowledge structures is presented in the next section.

Disciplinary knowledge structures

Bernstein describes two forms of disciplinary knowledge structure, hierarchical and horizontal. Disciplines such as the natural sciences have predominantly hierarchical knowledge structures. These disciplines progress by integrating new knowledge with existing knowledge in order to "[…] create very general propositions and theories, which integrate knowledge at lower levels" (Bernstein 1999: 162). In contrast, disciplines with predominantly horizontal knowledge structures (such as the humanities) progress by developing new ways of describing the world — here it is the new perspectives offered by these new descriptive 'languages' that provide the development. These two types of knowledge structure have been represented by Martin (2011) in terms of an expanding triangle for hierarchical knowledge structures and an increasing range of languages for horizontal knowledge structures (Figure 1).

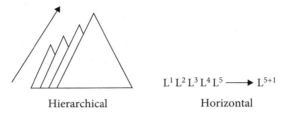

Hierarchical   Horizontal

Figure 1. Progression in hierarchical and horizontal knowledge structures. Adapted from Martin (2011: 42)

The work presented in this paper is representative of disciplines with hierarchical knowledge structures. The way in which disciplines with hierarchical knowledge structures develop is by incorporating more and more phenomena into the same explanatory system. This can be modelled in terms of widening the base of the triangle (to include more and more phenomena) and extending the apex — reaching ever-higher levels of integration and generalization.

A good illustration of the efficacy of Bernstein's hierarchical knowledge structures in the area of physics can be seen in the development of the discipline since 1900. In that year the Scottish physicist Lord Kelvin is (dis)credited with having proclaimed that "[t]here is nothing new to be discovered in physics now. All that remains is more and more precise measurement" (Davies & Brown 1988: 3–4). Whether or not Kelvin actually said those words, they are representative of the thinking at the time. In Bernstein's terms, the physicists of the day believed that the Newtonian hierarchical knowledge structure of physics was complete — new phenomena were expected to be subsumed within the existing structure of physics (analogous to simply expanding the base of the Newtonian triangle). Within just a few years these words proved to be incorrect with the inception of *two* new areas of physics that could not be explained by the existing Newtonian knowledge structure — quantum mechanics and general relativity. The relationship between these three knowledge structures can be seen in Figure 2 (Lindstrøm 2011).

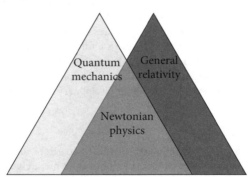

Figure 2. Hierarchical knowledge structures in physics. The relationship between Newtonian physics and the modern fields of quantum mechanics and general relativity. Adapted from Lindstrøm (2011).

Quantum mechanics and general relativity both subsume Newtonian physics; however, to date they have not been integrated with each other (Figure 3). Indeed, much of the work being carried out in modern theoretical physics today is concerned with the integration of these two discrete areas of physics into a single unified theory.

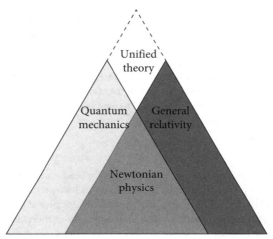

Figure 3. Searching for a unified theory. The as yet unexplained relationship between quantum mechanics and general relativity. Adapted from Lindstrøm (2011).

Bernstein singled out physics as the discipline with the most hierarchical knowledge structure. Kuteeva and Airey (under review) investigated PhD publication language and the frequency of teaching and research in English across a range of disciplines. They found that disciplines with hierarchical knowledge structures appear to have the least objection to the use of English, whilst disciplines with horizontal knowledge structures were much less likely to use English. The aim of this study then is to investigate physics lecturers' reflections on language use in their discipline as an exemplar of attitudes to language use in disciplines with hierarchical knowledge structures. What follows is an analysis of the attitudes of Swedish physics lecturers to language use in their discipline and their language-learning goals for their students.

Method

Setting and data collection

This paper compares the views of ten physics lecturers from four different Swedish universities. Two of the physics departments visited were in major traditional universities. Both of these had large student cohorts but differed somewhat in research tradition, one being more theoretical and the other more experimental. The other two physics departments were in more recently established universities with smaller departments and much fewer physics graduates. These smaller departments necessarily had more focus on 'service courses' in physics for engineers and trainee teachers at undergraduate level. Moreover there is a great difference in the student cohorts attracted at these universities, with the smaller departments mainly recruiting their students locally, whilst the larger departments attract students from the whole country and abroad. Thus it was hoped that the particularities of these very different settings would provide an opportunity to tease out different attitudes to English language use in a single discipline with a hierarchical knowledge structure.

The interviews analysed in this paper form part of a larger qualitative study into the disciplinary literacy goals of physics lecturers in Sweden and South Africa. A disciplinary literacy discussion matrix (Airey 2011b) was employed as the starting point for conducting in-depth, semi-structured interviews with ten physics lecturers from four Swedish universities. The matrix itself consisted of a list of representational resources, such as mathematics, graphs, diagrams, oral and written languages, etc. Lecturers were asked to indicate which resources they viewed as important for their students to learn to control, and the type of control desired for each resource — interpretive or generative. For example, with respect to the resource of written language, a lecturer expecting interpretive control would want students to be able to read the language, whilst expectations of generative control would refer to writing. The completed matrix then formed the basis for the interviews. In the interviews the lecturers were thus asked about the disciplinary language(s) and other forms of representation such as mathematics and graphs that they had indicated they would like their students to learn to control and their own attitudes to disciplinary language use. Interviews lasted approximately one hour and were conducted in English.

Data coding and analysis

The analysis presented in this paper draws on ideas from the phenomenographic research tradition. Phenomenography developed in Sweden in the 1970's as an interpretive methodology for educational research (Dall'Alba 1996). Informants' experiences of educational phenomena are examined through the analysis of interview material. Phenomenography is therefore particularly suited to the research reported here, since lecturers have been interviewed about their attitudes to English language use in the teaching and learning of their discipline.

One of the main axioms of phenomenography is that there is a limited number of ways in which a phenomenon may be experienced. The research takes a second-order approach where the words of informants are presented rather than those of the researcher (Trigwell 2000). In-depth interviews with a small purposeful sample of knowledgeable informants are thus central to the approach, with the researcher "working toward an articulation of the interviewee's reflections on experience that is as complete as possible" (Marton & Booth 1997: 130). The chosen informants should know the culture and be able to reflect on it and in words formulate to the interviewer what is going on (Merriam 1998). In phenomenography the use of quotations is essential as it shows the informants' contribution to the text, and maintains the second-order perspective.

Drawing on the phenomenographic notion of a "pool of meaning" (Marton & Booth 1997: 133) the qualitative analysis presented in this paper treats the interviews as a single data set. However, unlike phenomenographic research, the goal here was not to create an outcome space showing logical relations between qualitatively different ways of experiencing a phenomenon, but rather to simply document the expressed attitudes to language and the teaching and learning of physics that could be identified in the data.

Qualitative analysis involves "working with data, organizing it, breaking it into manageable units, synthesizing it, searching for patterns, discovering what is important and what is to be learned, and deciding what you will tell others" (Bogdan & Biklen 1992: 145). In this type of work iterative cycles are made through the data looking for patterns and key events. Each cycle results in loosely labelled categories that may then be split up, renamed or amalgamated in the next iteration. In this spirit, the data analysis proceeded as follows. First, the complete data set was worked through several times noting any sections that seemed important. Next, each of these sections was sorted into groups under tentative themes and any section that could not be immediately sorted this way was placed in a separate "miscellaneous" group. Each section of this miscellaneous group was then examined to decide whether the data constituted a new theme in itself, whether it could be combined with other data by amending the original themes, or whether in retrospect this was not something that should be included. This process continued until saturation was reached — the point where themes appear to stabilize and no new themes emerge. The complete data was then re-examined in order to check the themes against the original data and in an attempt to identify anything that had been missed that could be a potential theme. This process resulted in the identification of six themes.

Results and discussion

Analysis of the interview data suggested that there were indeed differences between lecturers in the different settings in how they viewed their students. Lecturers in the smaller universities seemed to see their students as future teachers or engineers, whilst those in the larger universities seemed to view their students exclusively as future physicists — even though there would probably be a fair proportion of engineers and teachers in their classes. This division led to lecturers at the larger universities using a larger proportion of English language disciplinary materials due to an emphasis on physics for the academy. Conversely, lecturers at the smaller universities used mainly Swedish, matching the societal needs of future practicing engineers and teachers. This analysis led to the conclusion that setting and student type do indeed affect the language goals of physics lecturers. However, further analysis showed that instead of focusing on the differences between institutions, the interview data could in fact be better explained with reference to the discipline of physics itself and its hierarchical knowledge structure.

Lecturers at all universities expressed the belief that the choice of language of instruction was not an issue for them — they preferred English, but Swedish could of course be used at early undergraduate levels. Initially, because the programmes at the smaller universities did not extend to physics at masters level, the actions of the lecturers on these programmes appeared to suggest they favoured Swedish as a teaching language. However when the level of the lecturers' courses was taken into account (introductory undergraduate versus advanced undergraduate/masters), this apparent difference could be seen to be unimportant — the lecturers at all four universities expressed quite similar attitudes to disciplinary language use. Thus, the similarities of the physics lecturers' attitudes across all four universities became the focus of interest for this study rather than the initial, face-value differences that could be explained by reference to teaching level and student type. So, whilst there were indeed differences across settings in terms of what was taught and in which language, these differences were on the whole understandable. What became interesting then were not the differences, but rather the striking similarities between the physics lecturers' expressed views. The analysis resulted in six interrelated themes that appear to hold for the physics lecturers' expressed views across all four universities:

1. Everyone needs the same introductory physics.
2. Progression in physics is important.
3. Physics is more than the sum of its representations.
4. Only English is used at higher levels.
5. I don't teach language.
6. Students need help with the 'language' of mathematics.

1. Everyone needs the same introductory physics

At lower levels students from physics, engineering and teacher training programmes are generally all taught together; however, the lecturers suggest that this is not problematic because *the physics is the same.*

(1) Interviewer: Do you have different goals for physicists and engineers?
    Lecturer: Yes, I suppose… but only slightly different.
    Interviewer: And for the teachers is it the same?
    Lecturer: Yes, I don't really distinguish between them. You need to understand
                 physics to be able to teach it.

This theme can be interpreted as seeing physics as something that is decontextualized and therefore valid in multiple settings. A consequence of this approach is that if language-learning goals are different for the different cohorts of students who are taking the same course (engineers, physicists, trainee teachers, etc.) then some sort of compromise must take place.

(2) Interviewer: So are all the books in English?
    Lecturer: Er, No. Unfortunately. There are so many good English books but we have
                 to teach the same course to trainee teachers, physicists and engineers and
                 the engineering programme demands Swedish literature.
                 And I think people would be better engineers if they were able to read this
                 kind of stuff in English.

In this last statement we can also see that there is a belief that working in English would have beneficial effects for students. Students at the larger universities read the same physics as those in smaller institutions, but the language of instruction is more likely to be English at the larger institutions. This belief that English is more useful than Swedish is further discussed in theme 4 below.

The notion that everyone needs the same physics is an interesting one — lecturers seem to want students to be able to understand physics in the same way that a physicist does — despite the fact that the majority of students will never become professional physicists. From an educational perspective there is a practical benefit of this approach — physics majors, engineering majors and trainee teachers can all attend the same lecture. The negative aspect of having many different types of students in the same lecture is that it leaves students to make the links to their particular area of application for themselves. As disciplinary experts the lecturers themselves have no difficulty seeing the links between their decontextualised, descriptions of physics and the students' particular specialisations, but it is unclear whether students can spontaneously make these links for themselves.

2.   Progression in physics is important

The lecturers in this study emphasised that course goals are always focused on what comes next in physics. This appears to be because they (like Bernstein) view physics as hierarchical — each stage depends on mastering the previous one.

(3) Interviewer: We are interested in how you decide on the learning goals for your
                 students…
    Lecturer: Physics has been around for a long time, you know it changes very slowly,
                 anyway I would say that that is much given by the next level what you need
                 to, to go on in physics.

From a CLIL perspective, this theme could explain why the larger universities in this study use more English in the teaching of physics — they could quite simply be projecting forward to the master's level where physics is conducted exclusively in English. Similarly, in the smaller universities where it is not possible to read physics at the master's level, physics would be allowed to be taught exclusively in Swedish. At first glance this argument would appear to be equally applicable to other disciplines with more horizontal knowledge structures. However, Bernstein (1999) suggested that these disciplines progress by creating new ways of describing the world and that this description is inevitably bound up with language. In physics, meaning is taken as agreed and shared across contexts, thus movement between languages entails translation between two equivalent terminologies. In the humanities, however, meaning is contested. Here, moving between languages may entail loss of precision — terms may not exist or have slightly different meanings in another language. In extreme cases the meanings made in one language may not be possible to construe in another (see Bennett 2010 for further discussion of this argument).

3.   Physics is more than the sum of its representations

All the lecturers mentioned at some stage in the interviews a belief that physics is more than the sum of its parts. This is expressed succinctly when a lecturer was asked about the relationship between languages and physics:

> (4)   These are tools, physics is something else. Physics is more than the sum of these tools it's the way physicists think about things — a shared reference of how to analyse things around you.

I interpret this excerpt as referring to the hierarchical nature of the physics disciplinary knowledge structure. The idea that physics is more than the sum of its representations has been discussed theoretically by Lemke (1998) in terms of multiplying meaning. This notion can be illustrated by using a numerical analogy. A linear system assumes there is a direct relationship between the disciplinary representational resources available and the knowledge these resources represent. If we take for instance the numbers two and four we can think of this in terms of $2 + 4 = 6$ (where two and four are the representational resources and 6 is the knowledge that they together create). Lemke rejects this view of meaning making, claiming that meaning, far from being linear, is in fact multiple. Thus, using the same example, Lemke suggests $2 \times 4 = 8$. For each extra resource that is introduced the differences between the two systems becomes even more striking. For example, by introducing the resource three to the linear system we get $2 + 4 + 3 = 9$ but in the multiple system we get $2 \times 4 \times 3 = 24$. I suggest another way of conceptualising the non-linear properties of representations, namely in terms of an emergent property of a complex system. In this way of thinking a certain combination of representational resources would give rise to something more than the individual parts. From an educational perspective this final way of viewing meaning making has been discussed by Airey and Linder (2009) in terms of knowledge being made available to students when they become fluent in a critical constellation of disciplinary representations.

> (5)   Interviewer: But teachers might have to read a book in English and then have to teach in Swedish...
>
>   Lecturer: Somehow I have the impression that this occurs quite naturally. That's not an issue I think.

A potential problem can be discerned here. A lecturer who understands physics sees no difficulty in changing languages — the physics meaning that she or he intimately understands in one language does not change simply because it is represented in another language. In a pedagogical setting, however, we are trying to help students understand the physics. It seems reasonable to assume that students would have lower barriers to understanding in L1 Swedish than in L2 English.

4.   Only English is used at higher levels

The feeling of the lecturers was that good physics books in Swedish are difficult to come by. This problem is exacerbated at higher levels where Swedish terminology sometimes does not exist. Swedish can therefore only be used in introductory-level courses:

(6) a.   The first 4 courses have books in Swedish.
     b.   The higher up you go the more English is involved.
     c.   The first 30 credits have books in Swedish after that it's mostly English.
     d.   We actually have a line in the course plan that says that the course can be taught in
          English if necessary.

For the whole cohort of physics lecturers, teaching either in English or in Swedish was not their
main preoccupation since the content (i.e. physics) is the same. The problem is rather that there is
insufficient terminology in Swedish at higher levels.

(7) a.   It becomes more dominated by the English language the higher up you go. More
          and more concepts the higher up you go are the more recent developed physics
          and somehow you know the translation of concepts erm — my impression is it has
          actually ceased. In particle physics for example there are a lot of words in physics
          that have not been translated. Sometimes they are possible to pronounce in a
          Swedish way. There was a Swedish translation proposed for a *Gluon* actually: *Limon*.
          Glue in Swedish is *lim* but it was never come into use.
     b.   As a lecturer in physics it's sometimes difficult to know how to express it in Swedish
          because English is really the professional language for physicists.

The fact that physics is the same whichever language one uses does not mean that physicists are
happy to use any language. Physics is an international endeavour and the publication of research is
entirely in English. The disciplinary discourse of physics is in English and given the choice physics
lecturers will prefer this language.

5.   I don't teach language
The lecturers expected their students to accomplish complex physics meanings with language but
they do not seem to think it is their job to teach this language. The lecturers insisted that they would
correct their students' Swedish but they would not feel confident correcting their English — this is a
side issue however because the lecturers claim "I don't teach language I teach physics".

(8) a.   Language is not mentioned in the syllabus.
     b.   The syllabus has more general physics goals there is no mention of language.
     c.   There is nothing about language skills in the syllabus.

These quotes are somewhat surprising given that two languages are often used interchangeably in
the teaching of undergraduate physics.

(9) Interviewer: Do you see yourself as a teacher of disciplinary Swedish or English?
     Lecturer: No, only in a very broad sense. Physics is a way of looking at nature and
                   understanding things in simplified models. These other things are for
                   presenting this way of thinking.

In an earlier study, Airey (2011a) investigated the attitudes and practices of Swedish university lecturers across a range of disciplines with respect to the correction of their students' English. Here too,
the lecturers reported that they would not feel comfortable correcting students' English.
     One lecturer took this physics focus even further by claiming he sees himself as neither a lan-
guage teacher nor a physics teacher:

(10) Lecturer: To me it's important that I'm not a physics teacher but I'm a teaching physicist. I want to stay curious and learn more about physics and continue to use all the tools of a physicist.

     Interviewer: You teach in Swedish but you have an English book — how do you think about the movement backwards and forwards between those?

     Lecturer: I don't think it's a big thing actually. I cannot say that I test them or train them in English. Of course they can always come and ask me, but I don't think that I take responsibility for training them in English. I don't correct their work in English.

One possible reason for the lecturers' reticence to teach language may be that they do not view language as the main method of meaning making in physics — rather mathematics is seen as a much more important disciplinary resource (see below).

6.   Students need help with the 'language' of mathematics

Although the lecturers would not take responsibility for their students' language skills, they did appear to think that it is their job to teach the 'language' of mathematics. This may be due to the relatively larger emphasis placed on mathematics in physics — mathematics is seen as better describing physical phenomena than written or oral text. Mathematics is also regarded as the most accurate representation of physics knowledge (Brookes & Etkina 2007). Therefore ideally students need to be as fluent as possible in this 'language'. All lecturers stated that this is something that they are prepared to help students with. Movement from the language of mathematics to either Swedish or English is seen as involving some loss in focus — the mathematics is the best description:

(11) a. You have to have mathematics in physics.

     b. Graphs, diagrams and mathematics they are some kind of erm (pause) to me they are a language. Er, But when I, when I talk to you I use this language but I want you to understand more and of course I want these things to confirm each other. I want these things to confirm the same picture.

     c. So English er, they they have very good language skills they have some problems in in the background in mathematics sometimes which is a problem so that we have to adapt the courses or make additions to the courses to help them out.

     d. I think that the problem is if you only see some, some other explanation than the mathematics you are not seeing the whole theory. Mathematics in quantum mechanics is the theory you are working on and it seems to work very well so we don't feel limited by the mathematics. The thing is that to be able to express it in a precise enough way you need mathematics. Language is more limited than mathematics in this case. So they need to use mathematics to see physics rather than language in this case.

So, although lecturers insisted that they were not language teachers, they were prepared to take responsibility for teaching the 'language of mathematics'. They seemed to suggest that mathematics is both less well developed in students and more central to physics meaning making than language(s).

Conclusions

I started this paper by claiming that all teachers are language teachers, and I chose to use theme 5 ("I don't teach language") for the title of the paper as a whole. This is because I concluded that this view, more than the others, expressed the essence of the respondents' thinking about their use of English. The physics lecturers in this study appear to view the choice of language of instruction as relatively unproblematic. This may in part be due to the insistence that only mathematics provides an accurate representation of physics knowledge. Following Kuteeva and Airey (under review), it is also claimed that this belief may be due to the hierarchical nature of physics knowledge structures, which are predicated on the development of universally agreed terminology across contexts. In hierarchical knowledge structures meaning is expected to be identical across languages (see Halliday 1993 for a comparison of English and Chinese scientific writing). Movement between languages involves translation of agreed, well-defined concepts and thus focuses purely on terminology rather than the translation of more complex stylistic, syntactic and lexico-grammatical features. Thus, one of the initial areas of interest for the study — the fact that courses may change teaching language from term to term — is not seen as a particularly problematic issue by the physics lecturers themselves.

I believe there is a potential risk in this approach, since students are essentially being left to work out the rules of physics discourse (in two languages) for themselves. At best the lecturer may be a discourse model for the students (in one language) but like Northedge (2002) I would argue that what students really need is the lecturer as a discourse guide (in both languages). Although the coining of new Swedish terminology in physics may have ceased (as suggested by one of the lecturers), there is still a strong Swedish physics discourse. Thus, students who learn physics in English risk code mixing English terms into their Swedish disciplinary discourse even when well-established Swedish terms do exist. In an earlier study I summarized the problem as follows:

> Until lecturers see their role as one of socialising students into the discourse of their discipline, there can be no discussion of the discursive goals of parallel language education. Without such a discussion lecturers will continue to insist that they are not language teachers and that this should be a job for someone else. (Airey 2011a: 50)

The findings presented here may be generalizable both within Sweden and internationally to other disciplines with hierarchical knowledge structures (such as the natural sciences). In future work it would be interesting to test this hypothesis by conducting similar research in another country. Clearly, though, the picture presented here should not be seen as representative of the wider linguistic situation in Swedish higher education, particularly in disciplines where different (more horizontal) knowledge structures are at work (e.g. arts, humanities, some vocational degrees and to some extent social sciences). In this respect it would be useful to conduct similar studies in Sweden with lecturers from disciplines with more horizontal knowledge structures to find out how these lecturers view language in their disciplines.

Finally, I would like to address the wider implications that the results reported here may potentially have for mainstream CLIL cooperation between content lecturers and language/educational specialists. I suggest that in subject areas with hierarchical knowledge structures, content lecturers may not view the choice of language of instruction as a particularly important issue. As explained above, this belief can be seen to stem from the expectation that disciplinary knowledge does not change when the language used to describe it changes. It seems reasonable to assume that a cooperating language/education specialist will typically come from a discipline with a more horizontal knowledge structure. There is potential for misunderstanding and conflict here, and I believe there is much to be gained if each party can understand the ontological and epistemological assumptions of the other. The content lecturer needs to appreciate that meanings she/he takes for granted are actually not self-evident and unambiguous *per se*. Rather it is the work that has been done in coordinating knowledge through the discipline's order of discourse (Fairclough 1995; New London Group 2000) that creates this situation. These discourse patterns need to be learned, and are often particularly problematic for undergraduate students (see Middendorf & Pace 2004, for a good discussion of this problem). Similarly, the language/educational specialist needs to appreciate that within a discipline with hierarchical knowledge structures, language and meaning may not be viewed as particularly problematic. Indeed, in the natural and applied sciences language may not even be viewed as the primary disciplinary meaning making resource. In such cases, a disciplinary outsider should not be surprised if the insider puts a greater emphasis on training and disambiguating other modes of representation (such as mathematics and graphs).

Acknowledgement

The research presented in this paper has been made possible by funding from the Swedish Research Council.

References

Airey, J. 2009. Science, Language and Literacy. Case Studies of Learning in Swedish University Physics. Acta Universitatis Upsaliensis. Uppsala Dissertations from the Faculty of Science and Technology 81. Uppsala.

Airey, J. 2010. The ability of students to explain science concepts in two languages. *Hermes — Journal of Language and Communication Studies* 45: 35–49.

Airey, J. 2011a. Talking about teaching in English. Swedish university lecturers' experiences of changing their teaching language. *Ibérica* 22: 35–54.

Airey, J. 2011b. The Disciplinary Literacy Discussion Matrix: A heuristic tool for initiating collaboration in higher education. *Across the disciplines* 8, ⟨http://wac.colostate.edu/atd/clil/index.cfm⟩ (19 September 2012)

Airey, J. & Linder, C. 2006. Language and the experience of learning university physics in Sweden. *European Journal of Physics* 27: 553–560.

Airey, J. & Linder, C. 2007. Disciplinary learning in a second language: A case study from university physics. In *Researching Content and Language Integration in Higher Education*, R. Wilkinson & V. Zegers(eds), 161–171. Maastricht: Maastricht University.

Airey, J. & Linder, C. 2008. Bilingual scientific literacy? The use of English in Swedish university science programmes. *Nordic Journal of English Studies* 7: 145–161.

Airey, J. & Linder, C. 2009. A disciplinary discourse perspective on university science learning: Achieving fluency in a critical constellation of modes. *Journal of Research in Science Teaching* 46(1): 27–49.

Benelux Bologna Secretariat. 2007–2010. *The official Bologna process website,*July 2007 — June 2010, ⟨http://www.ond.vlaanderen.be/hogeronderwijs/bologna/⟩ (19 September 2012)

Bennett, K. 2010. Academic discourse in Portugal: A whole different ballgame? *Journal of English for Academic Purposes* 9(1): 21–32.

Bernstein, M. 1999. Vertical and horizontal discourse: An essay. *British Journal of Sociology Education* 20: 157–173.

Björkman, B. 2010. Spoken lingua franca English at a Swedish technical university: An investigation of form and communicative effectiveness. Unpublished PhD thesis, Stockholm University.

Bogdan, R. C. & Biklen, S. R. 1992. *Qualitative Research for Education: An Introduction to Theory and Methods.* Boston: Allyn and Bacon.

Bolton, K. & Kuteeva, M. 2012. English as an academic language at a Swedish university: parallel language use and the 'threat' of English. *Journal of Multilingual and Multicultural Development* 33(5): 429–447.

Brookes, D.T. & Etkina, E. 2007. Using conceptual metaphor and functional grammar to explore how language used in physics affects student learning. *Physical Review Special Topics — Physics Education Research* 3: 1–16.

Calderhead, J. 1981. Stimulated recall: A method for research on teaching. *British Journal of Educational Psychology* 51: 211–217.

Dall'Alba, G. 1996. Reflections on phenomenography — an introduction. In *Reflections on Phenomenography: Toward a Methodology?*, G. Dall'Alba & B. Hasselgren (eds), 7–18. Gothenburg: ActaUniversitatisGothoburgensis.

Davies, P. & Brown, J. 1988. *Superstrings: A Theory of Everything?* Cambridge: Cambridge University Press.

Ekholm, B. & Bennet, C. 2011. Sverige har förlorat nio av tio utomeuropeiska studenter [Sweden has lost 9 out of 10 non-European students]. In *Dagens Nyheter*. Stockholm.

Falk, M. 2001. *Domänförluster i svenskan* [Domain losses in Swedish]. Nordic Council of Ministers.

Fairclough, N. 1995. *Critical Discourse Analysis*. London: Longman.

Gunnarsson, B.-L. & Öhman, K. 1997. *Det internationaliserade universitetet. En studie av bruket av engelska och andra främmande språk vid Uppsala universitet* [The Internationalized University. A Study of the Use of English and Other Foreign Languages at Uppsala University]. TeFa 16. Uppsala: Institutionen för nordiska språk, Uppsala universitet.

Halliday, M.A.K. 1993. The analysis of scientific texts in English and Chinese. In *Writing Science: Literacy and Discursive Power*, M.A.K. Halliday & J.R. Martin (eds), 124–132. London: Palmer Press.

Hincks, R. 2010. Speaking rate and information content in English lingua franca oral presentations. *English for Specific Purposes* 29: 4–18.

Höglin, R. 2002. *Engelska språket som hot och tillgång i Norden* [The English Language as Threat and Resource in the Nordic Countries.].vol. 561: TemaNord. Köpenhamn: Nordiska ministerrådet.

Josephson, O. 2005. Parallellspråkighet [parallel language use]. *Språkvård* 2005: 3.

Karlgren, J. & Hansen, P. 2003. Cross-language relevance assessment and task context. Paper presented at *Advances in Cross-Language Information Retrieval. Third Workshop of the Cross-Language Evaluation Forum, CLEF 2002*. Rome, Italy.

Kuteeva, M. & Airey, J. under review. Disciplinary differences in the use of English in higher education: Reflections on recent language policy developments. *Higher Education*.

Lemke, J.L. 1990. *Talking Science: Language, Learning and Values*. Norwood, NJ: Ablex.

Lemke, J.L. 1998. Multiplying meaning: Visual and verbal semiotics in scientific text. In *Reading Science: Critical and Functional Perspectives on Discourses of Science*, J.R. Martin and R. Veel (eds), 87–113. London: Routledge.

Lindstrøm, C. 2011. Analysing knowledge and teaching practices in physics. Presentation 21 November 2011. Department of Physics and Astronomy Uppsala University, Sweden.

Martin, J.R. 2011. Bridging troubled waters: Interdisciplinarity and what makes it stick. In *Disciplinarity*, F. Christie & K. Maton (eds), 252–264. London: Continuum.

Marton, F. & Booth, S. 1997. *Learning and Awareness*. Mahwah, NJ: Lawrence Erlbaum.

Melander, B. 2005. Engelska och svenska vid Uppsala universitet — en uppföljning. [English and Swedish at Uppsala University — a follow-up report]. In *Text i arbete/Text at Work Festskrift till Britt-Louise Gunnarsson den 12 januari 2005*, 135–143. Uppsala: Institutionen för nordiska språk, Uppsala universitet.

Merriam, S.B. 1998. *Qualitative Research and Case Study Applications in Education* (2nd ed.). San Francisco: Jossey-Bass Publishers.

Middendorf, J. & Pace, D. 2004. Decoding the disciplines: A model for helping students learn disciplinary ways of thinking. *New Directions for Teaching and Learning* 98 (Summer 2004): 1–12.

New London Group. 2000. A pedagogy of multiliteracies designing social futures. In *Multiliteracies: Literacy Learning and the Design of Social Futures*, B. Cope & M. Kalantzis (eds), 9–37. London: Routledge.

Northedge, A. 2002. Organizing excursions into specialist discourse communities: A sociocultural account of university teaching. In *Learning for Life in the 21st Century. Sociocultural Perspectives on the Future of Education*, G. Wells & G. Claxton (eds), 252–264. Oxford: Blackwell.

Pecorari, D., Shaw, P., Irvine, A. & Malmström, H. 2011. English for academic purposes at Swedish universities: Teachers' objectives and practices. *Ibérica* 22: 55–77.

Salö, L. 2010. *Engelska eller svenska? En kartläggning av språksituationen inom högre utbildning och forskning* [English or Swedish? A Survey of the Language Situation in Higher Education and Research]. Stockholm: Språkrådet.

Shaw, P. & McMillion, A. 2008. Proficiency effects and compensation in advanced second-language reading. *Nordic Journal of English Studies* 7: 123–143.

Söderlundh, H. 2004. Lika bra på engelska? En undersökning av hur studenter i Sverige förstår kurslitteratur på svenska resp. engelska [Just as good in English? A study of Swedish students' understanding of course texts in Swedish and in English]. *Språk och stil* 14: 137–165.

Söderlundh, H. 2010. Internationella universitet — lokala språkval [International University — local language choice], Uppsala: Institutionen för nordiska språk universitet, Uppsala universitet.

Swedish National Agency for Higher Education. 2008. *En högskola i världen — internationaliseringen för kvalitet* [Swedish Universities and Globalization — Internationalisation for Quality]. Stockholm: Högskoleverket.

Teleman, U. 1992. Det svenska riksspråkets utsikter i ett integrerat Europa [The outlook for Swedish in an integrated Europe]. *Språkvård* 1992: 7–16.

Trigwell, K. 2000. Phenomenography: Discernment and variation. In *Improving Student Learning: Improving Student Learning through the Disciplines*, C.Rust (ed), 75–85. Oxford: Oxford Brookes University, Oxford Centre for Staff and Learning Development.

Wächter, B. & Maiworm, F. 2008. *English-Taught Programmes in European Higher Education. The Picture in 2007*. Bonn: Lemmens.

Wickman, P.-O. & Östman, L. 2002. Learning as discourse change: A sociocultural mechanism. *Science Education* 86: 601–623.

Author's affiliation and e-mail address

Linnæus University and Uppsala University, Sweden

john.airey@lnu.se

English-medium programmes at Austrian business faculties

A status quo survey on national trends and a case study on programme design and delivery

Barbara Unterberger

Internationalisation processes have accelerated the implementation of English-medium programmes (EMPs) across European higher education institutions. The field of business and management studies has been particularly affected by this trend (Wächter & Maiworm 2008: 46) with numerous new EMPs introduced each year. This paper presents key findings of a quantitative status quo survey on the spread of EMPs across Austrian business faculties as well as those of a qualitative case study on English-taught programmes at Vienna University of Economics and Business (WU). The macro data regarding degrees, implementation years and entry requirements confirm trends identified by precedent studies: There are no English-taught BA programmes, nearly 30% of all programmes were implemented at the peak of the Bologna reforms and there is no uniform admission policy. On the micro level, the study identifies key facts concerning the curriculum design of EMPs. The results point towards a lack of awareness of the ESP (English for Specific Purposes) element in English-medium business education, as only 11% of the courses can be classified as ESP. Despite the lack of focus on ESP, the analysis also shows that about a third of all content classes explicitly state language learning aims in their course descriptions.

Introduction

The past decade has profoundly shaped European higher education as the Bologna agreement aimed at standardising the higher education systems of the 45 signatory countries (European Ministers of Education 1999; Benelux Bologna Secretariat 2007–2010). This 'harmonisation' of Europe's higher education has increased the mobility of students, researchers and teaching staff within the European Higher Education Area (EHEA) (Knight 2008: 22–24). Consequently, these internationalisation processes, and especially the introduction of the three-cycle degree structure (i.e. BA, MA and PhD), have led to an increase in the implementation of English-taught degree programmes (Wächter & Maiworm 2008: 52). The discipline of business and management studies has been particularly affected by this trend (Wächter & Maiworm 2008: 46), which is reflected in the increasing number of English-medium programmes (EMPs) that are implemented each year in this field of study. Despite this growth trend, there is still a lack of awareness of what the implementation of EMPs entails at both organisational and pedagogical levels. Precedent studies in the field of English-medium

AILA Review 25 (2012), 80–100. DOI 10.1075/aila.25.06unt
ISSN 1461–0213 / E-ISSN 1570–5595 © John Benjamins Publishing Company

teaching have produced valuable insights into the effects of using English as the medium of instruction in higher education (e.g. Airey 2009; Dafouz Milne & Núñez Perucha 2010; Hellekjaer 2010; Klaassen 2001; Smit 2010b). At the same time, however, there is still a lack of research evidence regarding fundamental aspects of programme design and development. For instance, more research is needed with regards to the organisational difficulties which arise when EMPs are implemented. Similarly, quality assurance issues concerning the curricula, staff and students of these programmes need to be addressed. The project presented in this paper strives to contribute to filling this research gap by providing a complete overview of the spread of EMPs at Austrian business faculties, the varying entry requirements and distinctive features in programme design and delivery. The study also intends to raise awareness of these critical issues among programme designers and, ultimately, promote the development of institutional policies. More precisely, the research project presented in this paper pursues three objectives:

1. to provide a complete overview of the spread of English-medium programmes at Austrian business faculties,
2. to give a detailed account on entry requirements, and
3. to uncover distinctive features in programme design and delivery.

The first part of the paper introduces the main research questions underlying the study and provides an overview of the project's three phases of data collection, Moreover, it also describes how other empirical studies on the topic of English-medium teaching in higher education have inspired and informed the present study. The second section presents the key findings of a status quo survey on English-medium programmes at Austrian business faculties. This includes an analysis of distribution patterns, implementation years and entrance requirements. The third section of the paper is concerned with the main findings of a case study on programme design and delivery at Vienna University of Economics and Business (WU). The subsections in this part discuss the motives behind the introduction of English-taught programmes, their unique selling propositions, marketing strategies and student recruitment issues, as well as challenges regarding the implementation and operation of EMPs. An analysis of course descriptions sheds light on the ESP (English for Specific Purposes) element in the curriculum of English-medium programmes (i.e. the teaching of discipline-specific language skills) and reveals if language learning objectives are explicitly stated. Moreover, the content experts' perspectives on teaching in English, including delicate issues relating to their English proficiency, are also considered. The paper concludes with a discussion of the study's key findings.

Research design and methods

The three phases of data collection
In order to meet the three main objectives mentioned earlier, the study combines macro and micro perspectives which are reflected in the three phases of data collection. The quantitative basis of the study is provided by a status quo survey which examines the key facts about English-medium programmes in Austrian business studies. In this first phase, the total number of EMPs across Austrian business faculties in the academic year of 2011/12 was recorded, which revealed their overall distribution pattern and also showed which degree programmes (i.e. BA, MA or PhD) are most commonly introduced in English.[1] The status quo survey also captured the years of implementation of the programmes as well as the specific entry requirements students have to fulfil to gain admission. In order to expose and compare admission policies, entry criteria were systematically analysed to find out how universities verify if prospective students have sufficient English skills and also the

aptitude to succeed in the programme. It was therefore recorded which language and analytical test certificates are required in order to be granted admission to the programmes and if certain applicants are exempt from these requirements. In addition, the universities' plans to expand their offering of English-taught programmes were also recorded.

Concerning the data gathering procedure in the status quo survey, it has to be pointed out that although the term 'survey' inevitably triggers associations with questionnaires, this was not the research instrument employed here. Since large-scale questionnaire surveys often suffer somewhat disappointing response rates (Wächter & Maiworm 2008: 20), this method of data collection was considered unfit for the study since the aim was to capture the *exact* number of EMPs. The research strategy pursued instead was systematic and extensive internet searches to ensure that the entire of-fer of English-medium programmes at Austrian business faculties is documented. Where necessary, specific enquiries were additionally made to guarantee a complete picture.

Building on the survey, all English-medium MA programmes taught at WU in the academic year 2011/12 (n = 4) were examined in order to identify the different varieties of English-medium teaching that prevail in EMPs. Here the approach was an in-depth analysis of course descriptions with the aim of categorising compulsory courses according to teaching formats, expected learning outcomes, assessment criteria and teaching methodology. The prime objective was to reveal whether language learning aims are explicitly stated in the course descriptions and which language-related skills are expected to be acquired and developed in these programmes. The analysis of the course catalogue was also meant to shed light on how English-taught programmes are designed in terms of their course composition. For instance, this step involved calculating the percentage of compulsory ESP classes and identifying elements of language teaching in content classes. Moreover, it was deter-mined whether pre-sessional or bridging courses, which are meant to prepare students for the fresh challenges of the English-taught degree programmes, are offered. Here one can distinguish between classes which are supposed to help students to cope with the language-related demands of English-medium education and courses designed to adjust imbalances in prior disciplinary knowledge of the usually heterogeneous student groups (Wächter 2003: 18). In addition to recording these ESP or content preparatory courses, it was examined whether students are provided with language support accompanying the discipline-specific content classes taught through English. Furthermore, it was also considered whether English skills or other language proficiencies are explicitly mentioned as assessment criteria. The research instrument employed here is an adapted version (cf. Unterberger & Wilhelmer 2011) of Räsänen's categorisation of English-medium teaching in higher education (as described in Greere & Räsänen 2008: 7–8).

The status quo survey and the analysis of course descriptions informed the third phase of data collection, i.e. expert interviews with programme directors (n = 5) of all English-medium MA and PhD programmes taught in the academic year 2011/12 at WU.[2] The interviews covered a wide range of topics and the programme directors, who also teach in the programmes, shared their first-hand experience of designing, implementing and developing English-medium programmes at the EU's largest business university (WU — Vienna University of Economics and Business 2011). They readily provided detailed information about the motives behind the introduction, organisational difficulties as well as pedagogical and curricular particularities of English-taught programmes. Alongside significant aspects in programme development and delivery, they shared their views on student target groups, entry requirements and recruitment procedures. Delicate matters such as the English language proficiency of students and teaching staff and corresponding language support or training classes were also raised in the course of the interviews. Similarly, sensitive questions regarding active collaboration between subject experts and language specialists or the assessment of students' English skills by content experts were also addressed. Based on the findings of the course description analysis, questions regarding language learning aims were posed. The interviews also considered the wider higher education context as the programme directors were invited to illustrate how internationalisation processes are reflected in their programmes and which marketing efforts are necessary in order to keep up with competitors. Additionally, the interviewees were asked to rate their programmes' status within the institution and to describe how important the degree course is for the university's public profile. Throughout the interview the programme directors were encouraged to share criteria which, from their point of view, need to be met in order to guarantee the long-term success of an English-medium degree programme in business studies. Moreover, they made predictions for the future development and growth of English-medium programmes and also ventured their opinion on the rather controversial topic of the possible introduction of English-taught bachelor's programmes in Austria.

Research foundations

The overall design of this project, including its research aims and questions, was shaped and inspired by several precedent empirical studies which have been conducted on English-medium teaching in higher education. First and foremost, this study is profoundly influenced by the pioneering work of Maiworm and Wächter, who conducted two large-scale studies on the spread of English-taught degree programmes in all disciplines at European higher education institutions (2002; 2008). Their first extensive data collection in the year 2002 was followed by an even larger one in 2007, which allowed a direct comparison between the figures and a systematic assessment of the development of EMPs across Europe. The main distinguishing feature of their second survey was that only programmes *entirely* taught in English were included in the year 2007 (Wächter & Maiworm 2008: 9). The study presented in this paper followed suit by excluding programmes from the survey which are only partly taught in English. The topics explored in this project are, in general, largely based on the work of Maiworm and Wächter. Their findings regarding the motives behind the introduction of EMPs, student target groups, marketing strategies, quality assurance issues, etc. informed the majority of the present study's research questions.

As a starting point for the identification of the different types of English-medium teaching at the tertiary level, conceptual considerations (cf. Unterberger & Wilhelmer 2011) were derived from Greere's and Räsänen's LANQUA project report (2008).[3] Their categorisation of the various instructional types in English-medium settings (Greere & Räsänen 2008: 7–8), provided the basis for the analysis of individual courses in EMPs. In this context, Räsänen's and Fortanet-Gómez's survey on ESP and EAP (English for Academic Purposes) practices at universities in eight European countries was also particularly influential (2008b).

For the development of interview questions, a number of case studies on English-medium teaching at European institutions of higher education were important. For instance, Wilkinson's publications were a major inspiration, especially his examples of good practice and potential pitfalls drawn from over 25 years of English-medium education at Maastricht University (2008a; 2010a). His observations on the integration of content and language learning in higher education and the impact of the language of instruction on content teachers provided food for thought, particularly for the interviews with programme directors (2010b; 2005a). Similarly, a SWOT analysis conducted at the University of Helsinki by Lehtonen et al. (2009) triggered several interview questions regarding the effects of English-taught programmes on the stakeholders involved. When it comes to the delicate subject of the English proficiency of staff and students in EMPs, the findings of the case studies undertaken by Hellekjaer offer strong arguments especially regarding the necessity for language training and support (2007, 2010). Questions about teacher training were largely prompted by Klaassen's study on effective lecturing in English-medium education (2001) and by her report about Delft University of Technology actually testing the English language proficiency of its teaching staff (2010). The need for the professional development of lecturers which she identified (2008) also provided input for the interviews.

Results and discussion

Degree programmes and distribution patterns

As can be seen in Figure 1 below, 26 English-medium degree programmes were offered at Austrian business faculties in the academic year of 2011/12. The survey shows that EMPs can be found exclusively in the second and third cycles of the degree structure. Currently, 15 master's programmes and 11 PhD programmes have been implemented at these institutions. While it is not particularly surprising that most of the EMPs (i.e. 58%) are master's programmes, the high number of English-taught PhD programmes on offer is rather striking. Since PhD programmes were excluded from the large-scale surveys of Maiworm and Wächter (2008: 9), a basis for comparison is not provided. Still, given the fact that 42% of all EMPs at Austrian business faculties are classified as doctoral or PhD programmes, the institutions clearly aim at internationalising their third cycle programmes. The programme director of PhD programmes at WU stressed that these study courses are clearly intended to be truly international, that is, they strive for a mixed student body and also a culturally diverse faculty. The fact that established third cycle programmes are crucial for the inclusion in business school rankings and the increasing use of English in PhD theses (Räisänen & Fortanet-Gómez 2008a: 7) seem to have fostered this development.

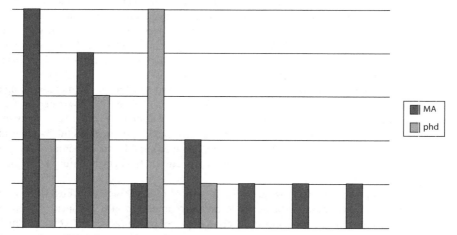

Figure 1. Overall distribution of EMPs at Austrian business faculties in the academic year of 2011/12

As expected, there are no bachelor's programmes which are entirely taught in English. This finding is in line with those of Maiworm and Wächter who also found that EMPs in Europe are "very predominantly offered in the second cycle" and that English-taught bachelor's programmes are rather rare, regardless of the discipline of study or type of institution (2008: 48). However, the interviews with the programme directors at WU revealed that English-medium BA programmes are actually very likely to be introduced. All interviewees agreed that first cycle programmes will definitely be affected by the English-medium trend in the near future and some indicated that this might even be a necessity. One programme director stressed that the current situation of bachelor's degrees being exclusively taught in German did not prepare WU students for the demands of the highly specialised English-medium master's programmes. As Austrian state universities are generally not supposed to impose entrance restrictions upon applicants at the BA level, the only prerequisite for most disciplines is a higher education entrance qualification (Eurydice 2010a: 61). Since WU has become severely overcrowded in recent years and English-medium programmes tend to attract large numbers of domestic and foreign students, university officials are hesitant when it comes to implementing English-taught BA programmes. Nevertheless, steps towards introducing an English track in the bachelor's programme have already been taken. One programme director argued that such an English track in the BA programme is absolutely necessary to boost the university's international reputation and attract highly qualified foreign students. Another pointed out that a bilingual programme, i.e. one that is partly taught in German and partly in English, would also have its merits as it would deter foreign students from enrolling in the programme (for the impact the introduction of study fees has had on overseas enrolments in Sweden cf. Airey, this volume). While attracting fewer students from abroad is usually considered a disadvantage (cf. Wilkinson 2008a: 172), the current situation at WU calls for measures to reduce prospective students. Moreover, the programme director suggested that such a partial EMP could start with a quarter of the courses taught through English in the first year and then gradually increasing the number of English-medium classes as the disciplinary knowledge taught moves from basic to specialisation. Another argument in favour of the introduction of EMPs at the BA level was brought up in the interviews, namely that domestic students who wish to apply for a master's programme abroad would be markedly better equipped for the challenges of studying through the medium of English. As a *quid pro quo*, English-medium bachelor's programmes can also enhance the quality of the English-taught master's degree courses as the university can then directly recruit the best BA students into the MA programme (cf. Wilkinson 2008a: 179).

The overall distribution pattern of EMPs across Austrian business faculties clearly identifies the University of Innsbruck and Vienna University of Economics and Business (WU) as the main providers of English-taught degree programmes in business and economics studies. Together they offer more than 54% of the EMPs currently implemented at Austrian business faculties. Both universities pride themselves on their fairly high positions according to various higher education rankings alongside prestigious business schools across the globe (University of Innsbruck 2011; Vienna University of Economics and Business 2011). Clearly, implementing English-medium programmes is a decisive factor for the inclusion in international university rankings (Times Higher Education World University Ranking; Leiden Ranking; Financial Times European Business School Ranking), as EMPs ensure international comparability and help to raise the institution's public profile (Wilkinson 2010a).

Implementation years
Turning to the statistics on implementation years of the EMPs across Austrian business faculties, Table 1 below shows that the longest running programme, *PhD Finance*, was introduced at WU in the academic year of 2005/06. The introduction of English-taught programmes in business studies reached its peak in the academic year of 2009/10 when more than 30% of all programmes which currently exist at Austrian universities were implemented. Both studies by Maiworm and Wächter (2002: 62; 2008: 51–52) came to the conclusion that EMPs are a rather young phenomenon and this observation also holds true for the present study. More than 65% of the EMPs currently implemented at Austrian business faculties have been set up in the last three years (since 2009/10). This boom most likely bears a causal relation to the official launch of the European Higher Education Area (EHEA) (European Ministers of Higher Education 2010) in 2010. While the results for the academic

year of 2011/12 might suggest a period of stagnation, the launch of several programmes in 2012/13 has already been announced. As a point of reference, 4 MA programmes and 1 PhD programme are about to be introduced in the academic year of 2012/13 at WU alone.

Table 1. Implementation years of EMPs at Austrian business faculties

Year of implementation	MA programmes	PhD programmes	University
2005/06		PhD Finance	Vienna University of Economics and Business (WU); (Vienna Graduate School of Finance); financed by the Austrian Science Fund FWF
2007/08	Production Science and Management		Graz University of Technology
2007/08	Organisation Studies		University of Innsbruck
2007/08	Strategic Management		University of Innsbruck
2007/08	Information Systems		University of Innsbruck
2007/08		Doctoral Programme Social and Economic Sciences (English track)	Vienna University of Economics and Business (WU)
2008/09	Banking and Finance		University of Innsbruck
2008/09	Applied Economics		University of Innsbruck
2008/09		PhD Program in Management	University of Innsbruck
2009/10	Quantitative Economics, Management, and Finance		University of Vienna
2009/10	International Management / CEMS		Vienna University of Economics and Business (WU)
2009/10	Quantitative Finance		Vienna University of Economics and Business (WU)
2009/10		PhD Program in Economics (Joint programme with Johannes Kepler University Linz)	University of Innsbruck
2009/10		PhD Program in Economics (Joint programme with University of Innsbruck)	Johannes Kepler University Linz
2009/10		Logistics and Operations Management	University of Vienna
2009/10		Statistics and Operations Research	University of Vienna

Table 1. (*continued*)

Year of implementation	MA programmes	PhD programmes	University
2009/10		Management	University of Vienna
2010/11	General Management		Johannes Kepler University Linz
2010/11	Strategy, Innovation, and Management Control		Vienna University of Economics and Business (WU)
2010/11	Supply Chain Management		Vienna University of Economics and Business (WU)
2010/11	Business Informatics		Vienna University of Technology
2010/11		PhD Finance	University of Vienna; (Vienna Graduate School of Finance); financed by the Austrian Science Fund FWF
2010/11		PhD Program in Economics	University of Vienna; (Vienna Graduate School of Economics); financed by the Austrian Science Fund FWF
2011/12	International Management		Alpen Adria University of Klagenfurt
2011/12	Global Business (Joint programme with University of Victoria and National Sun Yat-sen University Taiwan)		Johannes Kepler University Linz
2011/12		DIBT Doctoral Programme in International Business Taxation	Vienna University of Economics and Business (WU); financed by the Austrian Science Fund FWF

Entry requirements for EMPs

Universities' admission criteria for EMPs can generally be grouped into two broad categories: the first concerns the applicants' English proficiency and the second is meant to provide evidence of the aptitude and analytical skills of prospective students. While the Bologna reforms were primarily implemented to create transferability (Confederation of EU Rectors' Conference and the Association of European Universities (CRE) 2000:4), there is certainly no uniform admission policy for EMPs to be found, not even among the 7 universities investigated in the present study.

When analysing the admission criteria concerning the English proficiency of applicants, the following picture emerges: for more than 57% of all EMPs at Austrian business faculties, prospective students are required to submit a TOEFL or IELTS score in order to prove that their English skills reach an advanced level. This concerns 60% of the MA programmes and nearly 55% of the PhD programmes. The slightly lesser percentage of PhD programmes which request TOEFL or IELTS certificates from applicants indicates that PhD students are considered to have already developed advanced English skills.

On the whole, the majority of applicants are obliged to hand in a TOEFL or IELTS score, regardless of their country of origin. However, for about 11% of the programmes such standardised

English tests are only mandatory for students from outside the European Economic Area (EAA). This is a common strategy which is based on the assumption that students from the EU or EAA states possess the necessary English language skills to cope with the demands of English-medium instruction (Räisänen & Fortanet-Gómez 2008b: 43; Wilkinson 2008a: 174). Nevertheless, Hellekjaer (2010) tested the lecture comprehension of domestic and foreign students and his results suggest that both groups were experiencing difficulties in English lectures. Curiously, his results indicate that nearly a quarter of the surveyed Norwegian students also had problems following their L1 lectures (Hellekjaer 2010: 240). An earlier study revealed that two-thirds of Norwegian students did not reach band 6 (i.e. 'competent user') of the IELTS academic reading module (Hellekjaer 2009: 198). It can therefore be argued that IELTS or TOEFL tests should be mandatory for all students since "the standards of students entering higher education vary considerably both across and within countries" (Wilkinson 2005b). The minimum IELTS score required for nearly 80% of EMPs at Austrian business faculties is 7, while only one institution would accept an IELTS score of 6.5. Therefore, the results from the Norwegian students, who did not reach band 6 in the academic reading section, clearly indicate that it is necessary to test all applicants' English skills, including those of domestic students.

However, not all institutions request a certificate as proof of applicants' English language proficiency. Indeed, for more than 30% of the programmes no such proof needs to be submitted. Two of these programmes set out a certain final grade in the English school-leaving examination, i.e. not worse than 'satisfactory' (3) or 'good' (2) in accordance with the Austrian school grading system. The entrance criteria for two other programmes merely indicate that the English language proficiency of applicants needs to be at B2 level in accordance to the Common European Framework of Reference for Language (CEFR), which is the English level students are expected to have when they finish secondary education (Horak 2010: 20). Slightly more than 19% of the programmes also accept certificates of (Business) English classes taken at a tertiary level institution worth 14 to 15 ECTS credits, with a grade point average of 2 or 2.49. While the latter approach appears quite reasonable, especially if the classes taken focus on discipline-specific language skills, the strategy of accepting school-leaving certificates again points towards a lack of awareness regarding the necessary level of English proficiency to cope with the demands of English-medium instruction.

The second category of entrance requirements is supposed to prove the aptitude and analytical skills of prospective students and also comprises two firmly established tests which are frequently requested. On the one hand, this is the Graduate Management Admission Test (GMAT).[4] and on the other, the Graduate Record Examination (GRE).[5] At Austrian business faculties, 27% of the programmes require applicants to submit a GMAT or GRE score. In contrast to the TOEFL/IELTS situation described above, there are only about 8% of the programmes which exclusively ask applicants from non-EAA and non-EU countries to submit a GMAT or GRE score.

Whereas GMAT or GRE scores are internationally recognised tests, one Austrian institution introduced a tailor-made exam to ensure that prospective students meet the requirements of the programme. Prospective students of the MA Programme *International Management* at Alpen Adria University of Klagenfurt are supposed to sit an entrance examination. However, students who are able to present 24 ECTS credits in business or management studies do not have to take the exam. In this way, the entrance exam allows students with educational backgrounds other than business studies to enrol in the programme.

The interviews with the programme directors at WU revealed that the GMAT was a hotly debated topic in the past year as the university considered making it a standard requirement for all applicants of all English-medium programmes. While some programme directors thought that this would simplify the selection process and increase comparability of candidates, others feared that such a score could not accurately assess the suitability of applicants. Interviewees in favour of the GMAT argued that the programmes' students came from up to 60 different countries of origin and that the GMAT is therefore absolutely necessary to allow comparability between degrees. From their point of view, the GMAT thus also ensures fairness in the selection process. On the other hand, opponents of a mandatory GMAT stressed that due to the narrow specialisation of their programmes, they prefer to rely on letters of recommendation written by the applicants' previous supervisors, instructors or employers. Furthermore, if they encourage excellent WU students from the BA degree course to apply for the MA programme, they see no need to request a GMAT or GRE score. Since the possible introduction of a mandatory GMAT for all EMPs at WU fuelled such lively controversy, the university is not very likely to establish a uniform admission policy for all English-taught MA and PhD programmes. In this case it remains rather questionable as to whether it is actually worthwhile to strive for uniformity, since the programmes' specialisations and consequential target groups are so varied.

On the whole, one has to bear in mind that widespread standardised entrance tests such as TOEFL, IELTS, GMAT or GRE were originally developed for universities in English-speaking countries and "it is not certain that they are appropriate for EMI programmes in a non-English-speaking environment" (Wilkinson 2008a: 174). Therefore, when it comes to measuring the English proficiency of applicants, "this may even mean that higher, not lower entry requirements are necessary" (Wilkinson 2008a: 180). Maiworm and Wächter (2003: 21) even call for the development of a European proficiency test for the various disciplines, which uses the GMAT and GRE as models but meets the demands of non-English speaking settings.

Motives behind the introduction of English-medium programmes
One of the central topics covered in the interviews with the programme directors at WU was the underlying reasons for introducing English-medium MA and PhD programmes. Maiworm and Wächter included this question in both of their surveys and came to somewhat different results (2002: 12; 2008: 67). While they found that the main motive was "to attract international students who would not enrol in a programme taught in the domestic language" (Wächter & Maiworm 2008: 67), the WU programme directors hold a slightly divergent view on this subject. They expressed their belief that the choice of English as the medium of instruction is, on the one hand, a direct consequence of the very specific foci of their programmes and, on the other, a necessity to achieve the high standards of academic excellence they pursue. The interviewees also pointed out that most of the literature and textbooks for the narrowly specialised subjects of the programmes is published in English anyway and that their expertise in the field has been largely acquired through English. From their point of view, it is therefore only natural to set English as the medium of instruction. These findings indicate that in the context of WU, it is causally necessary that these programmes are taught through English in order to attract the intended target audience. Indeed, if the programmes were taught in German, their 'international' foci would stand in stark contrast to the language of instruction.

The concept of 'internationalisation at home' represents another striking difference. Maiworm and Wächter found that the motivation "to provide students with an international education" (Maiworm & Wächter 2002: 12) and "make domestic students 'fit' for the global labour markets" (Wächter & Maiworm 2008: 67) was the second most often cited reason to implement an English-medium programme across European higher education institutions. However, the programme directors at WU did not specifically mention 'internationalisation at home' as a principal reason for the introduction of their programmes. When they were asked explicitly about the aforementioned advantages to domestic students, they regarded it as a positive side effect rather than an underlying motivation. Regardless of whether it is considered a valuable spin-off or an intended outcome, domestic students can indeed profit from the heterogeneous student body which is usually established in these programmes:

> [EMPs] constitute a fruitful framework for internationalisation at home for those who cannot participate in student exchanges or other study-abroad/work-abroad programmes. The international atmosphere in [EMPs] helps expose people to and thus develop skills in international communication and foreign languages. It is often thought that these international encounters give rise to innovations and cooperation opportunities. (Lehtonen et al. 2009: 267)

Given that up to 70% of the students enrolled in the English-taught programmes at WU have a native tongue other than German, students can benefit from the multilingual and intercultural learning environment.

Unique selling propositions

When the programme directors were asked to describe the unique selling proposition (USP) of the EMPs, two key concepts were formulated repeatedly. The most frequently mentioned one was the notion of interdisciplinarity. According to the programme directors, the degree courses offer a unique blend of sub-disciplines as well as related subject areas. This interdisciplinary approach can be demonstrated by taking *Supply Chain Management* as an example. This MA programme combines the disciplines of production management, transport and logistics management, business administration, business informatics, geoinformatics and operations research. This combination is achieved by the collaboration of various WU departments. The programme's director pointed out that this interdisciplinary perspective certainly contributed to the success of the programme.

In general, interdisciplinarity appears to be a shared characteristic of EMPs, which has also been identified in other settings: "[EMPs] are more interdisciplinary: they cater for students with bachelor's degrees from various fields and have sometimes been established as a joint project between two or more faculties" (Lehtonen et al. 2009: 268).

The interdisciplinary design of EMPs is closely connected to the second most often cited USP, namely the specific foci of the programmes. As already indicated above, the interviewees emphasised that their programmes are 'unique', because they cover narrowly specialised subjects. This deliberate brand positioning is seen as a USP and it is in fact a WU policy to implement English-medium programmes which address very specific target audiences. According to Wilkinson (2008a: 179), universities should focus on "new niche ventures" and "endeavour to be a first-mover in the competitive market". Therefore, occupying a special niche within and across national borders can actually be regarded as a critical success factor of EMPs.

Marketing and student recruitment

The days in which marketing was considered inappropriate in academia are definitely over and as most universities want to attract a mixed group of domestic and foreign students, the programme designers need to define their target audiences in great detail (Wächter 2003: 13–14). Consequently, English-medium programmes require specific marketing strategies, not least because "fierce competition over international students has set in" (Wächter & Maiworm 2008: 15). If the students outside the target group are attracted in the introductory phase of an EMP, this is most likely because of wrong marketing (Maiworm & Wächter 2003: 14). Programme designers are therefore advised to "invest extensively in promotion activities, but fine-tune marketing to key target audience" (Wilkinson 2008a: 179).

The English-medium programmes at WU employ a very eclectic marketing mix which includes online strategies such as Google ad campaigns and also classic advertising efforts like participating in job fairs. While most of the promotional material is produced by the marketing department of WU, the programmes are also engaged in individual marketing efforts. Some programme directors emphasised that it was necessary to draw up specific marketing strategies, because the brochures for all EMPs at WU are identically designed and do not leave room to promote the distinguishing features of individual programmes. Since they are not supposed to change the way their programme is represented in these brochures, the directors felt that they need to introduce more target-specific marketing in order to attract the intended students. In one interview it was reported that the brochure might even discourage targeted audiences, because it simply does not fit the overall concept of the programme. Since the official promotional activities are often considered to be insufficient, student recruitment for nearly all of the EMPs at WU is now partly carried out via international networks of the faculty. The interviewees explained that in this way top students can be directly addressed by trusted colleagues. This method increased the intake of excellent students and also strengthened professional connections with domestic and international higher education institutions. Once the introductory phase is passed and the programmes produce their first graduates, the directors hope that word-of-mouth advertising will increase and an international reputation will be built up. Moreover, there are plans to use alumni's reviews and feedback to promote the programmes and also to build up an alumni network.

Challenges regarding the implementation and operation of English-medium programmes
When English-medium programmes are newly introduced in a university, several structural and organisational aspects need to be considered to ensure a smooth implementation and an efficient operation of these programmes. Therefore, coherent institutional strategies specifically for EMPs need to be developed and implemented, plus universities need to be flexible and willing to change (Maiworm & Wächter 2003: 20).

In the course of the interviews, the directors reflected upon the challenges they faced during the early stages of the programmes. For instance, the very first English-medium programme at WU (i.e. *CEMS — International Management*) was confronted with the situation that an admissions office needed to be established in order to manage applications. This is quite typical of the introductory phase of the first EMP which takes on a pioneering role. The establishment of new organisational units and the recruitment of new administrative staff are inevitable (Maiworm & Wächter 2003: 18–19). However, an admission office is not the only necessary division which needs to be created. Most interviewees reported that international students often struggle with their visas or encounter housing problems when they arrive. Currently, these matters are dealt with individually by the programmes' administrative staff as there is no centrally-operated WU unit which is responsible for such concerns. The interviews revealed that Erasmus or exchange students are very well taken care of, while there is no service facility where foreign students of the EMPs can seek advice. Additionally, these students should be introduced to the particularities of the host university as they might require guidance to adjust to the conventions of teaching and studying in a European university setting (Maiworm & Wächter 2003: 22). Lehtonen et al. (2009: 270) actually identified "the vague or non-existent orientation for incoming students" as one of the main weaknesses in their SWOT analysis of EMPs at the University of Helsinki.

Moreover, the programme directors indicated that establishing a truly bilingual university is not as straightforward as it might appear at first sight, because it concerns all parts of university administration. Important documents, websites and information materials need to be published in English and, most importantly, all staff need to be sufficiently fluent in English (cf. Maiworm & Wächter 2003: 22; Wilkinson 2008a: 176).

The ESP element in English-medium programmes
As already described above, one component of the present study is a systematic analysis of the course descriptions of all English-taught MA programmes at WU to shed light on central aspects of curriculum design. Table 2 below shows the overall course composition of the four English-medium MA programmes taught at WU in the academic year of 2011/12. The majority (i.e. 88%) of the compulsory courses are content classes in which English is used as the medium of instruction (EMI), while ESP classes account for 11%.

Table 2. Course composition of English-medium MA programmes at WU in 2011/12

Programme	EMI	pre-sessional EMI	ESP	pre-sessional ESP
International Management, CEMS	18	0	2	0
Quantitative Finance	18	1	2	1
Strategy, Innovation, and Management Control	12	0	3	0
Supply Chain Management	15	0	0	0
Totals	64		8	

The degree courses *Quantitative Finance* and *Strategy, Innovation, and Management Control* both introduced 3 ESP classes into their curricula and thus represent the highest proportion of ESP teaching in the programmes investigated. Programme designers of *Supply Chain Management*, on the other hand, did not include any ESP courses. In the interview it was emphasised that a focus on language simply did not match their strategic vision for the programme. This attitude suggests that there is a lack of awareness when it comes to the development of discipline-specific English skills. Previous research also indicates that content lecturers "may not have fully problematised questions like [...] what the desired level of disciplinary communicate competence [...] is and how this will be developed" (Airey 2011) within the programme.

Among the 72 compulsory classes of all English-taught MA programmes at WU, only two pre-sessional courses could be identified, both of which are meant to prepare students for the *Quantitative Finance* programme. Whereas the 'Bridging Course Finance' can be described as a classic ESP format in which students are introduced to the language of finance, the 'Bridging Course Mathematics' aims at adjusting imbalances in the students' prior disciplinary knowledge. The programme directors of the *Quantitative Finance* programme reported that although the two bridging courses might seem quite different, they share one similarity, namely the aim to familiarise the students with the terminology of business finance and mathematics, respectively. Although these two pre-sessional courses are considered to be excellent preparation for the programme, they did not trigger any spin-offs. On the contrary, the other programme directors deliberately did not include any pre-sessional classes in the curricula. One even argued that students who needed such preparation are simply not good enough to cope with the demands of the degree course.

However, the pre-sessional ESP course mentioned above could actually serve as a model of successful collaboration between content and language experts. In the WU context, it represents the effective cooperation between the Institute of English Business Communication and the Finance, Accounting and Statistics department. The decisive factor for the success of tailor-made language classes in EMPs is that the content experts set the disciplinary goals which then provide the basis for the language teachers' course design. In other words, "it is the content lecturers, rather than their discussion partners in languages [...], who must make the final decisions about the particular mix of communicative practices that is needed to achieve disciplinary literacy" (Airey 2011). In their survey on ESP and EAP practices at universities in eight European countries, Räisänen and Fortanet-Gómez (2008b) found that in the Netherlands and Sweden *all* ESP courses at the nine institutions surveyed resulted from close collaboration between content and language specialists. These tailor-made ESP classes take on an adjunct function since they "are closely linked to the content courses in that ESP teachers use the materials and tasks that the students are assigned in the content courses" (Räisänen & Fortanet-Gómez 2008b: 42). In terms of programme design, this probably represents the ideal context for ESP teaching in EMPs (cf. Wilkinson 2008b: 55). However, adjunct ESP courses remain exceedingly rare, not least because "the traditional watertight boundaries between academic fields are far more difficult to overcome" (Räisänen & Fortanet-Gómez 2008b: 22) than one would expect. Wilkinson observed that the diminishing proportion of ESP classes in EMPs might even be "an unforeseen side-effect of the Bologna process" (2008b: 56). In other words, the restructuring into the three-cycle degree structure often meant that elements included in the previous structure could no longer be integrated in the new BA and MA programmes. At Maastricht University this led to sharp cuts in ESP classes in its EMPs, which used to have a strong emphasis on the ESP element before the restructuring (Wilkinson 2008b: 56; for a somewhat different development in a Spanish university see Fortanet-Gómez, this volume).

The fact that only 11% of the courses can be classified as ESP indicates that the teaching and learning of subject-specific language skills is at most a side issue in programme design. The interviews revealed that language learning is frequently considered incidental (cf. Wilkinson 2010b) and that students' English proficiency is expected to be at a very high level when they are granted admission to the programme. The present study aims at increasing the awareness of the ESP element in EMPs among programme designers, because "students are not merely learning a discipline but also [...] the specific language of the discipline" (Wilkinson 2008a: 178).

Language learning objectives
The analysis of course descriptions also intended to reveal whether language learning objectives are explicitly stated and which language-related skills students are expected to develop in these programmes. This part of the study produced rather surprising results, as 32% of all content classes actually include explicit language learning aims. The most frequently formulated goals are to foster presentation, discussion and negotiation skills and to develop the students' academic reading and writing. Therefore, some of the widespread assumptions about English-medium teaching in higher education are challenged, namely that English merely fulfils a vehicular function and that language learning objectives are not actively pursued in EMPs (cf. Järvinen 2008: 78). In the interviews, the programme directors also confirmed these aims but stressed that some of them might be more important than others. The development of terminology knowledge is of great importance and thus also part of the assessment criteria. With the exception of the *CEMS — International Management* programme, negotiation and presentation skills are not explicitly assessed, although all of the interviewees stressed that when it comes to the grading of term papers and presentations, the students' language proficiency plays a role as well. One interviewee emphasised that even if content knowledge cannot be separated from language skills, he feels that he is not qualified to assess the latter and therefore tries to focus primarily on the quality of content in students' contributions. Here the question arises whether or not subject experts should be able to provide language feedback. Considering the very limited hours of ESP teaching shown above, it might even be a necessity to integrate language aspects into assessment criteria. Otherwise, "students may have grounds for complaint if they are not receiving advice on how to develop their language competences in the disciplines" (Wilkinson 2008a: 178).

Although the findings discussed in this section point towards some awareness concerning language learning objectives, they also suggest that content experts are "generally not aware of what the language learning aspect entails for their teaching" (Smit 2003: 47; for a more detailed discussion of such findings see Airey, this volume). Whether or not the stated language learning aims are actually fulfilled in the EMPs lies outside the scope of this study.

Teaching through English

Since all the interviewed directors also teach in their programmes and all of them are native speakers of German, they were asked to illustrate the difference between teaching in English and teaching in their mother tongue. They all argued that English as the medium of instruction is a natural choice for them, because it is the language they use in publications and conference talks. Moreover, it was also indicated that the main body of literature on their subjects is published in English and it would thus increase the amount of effort required to teach it in German. While several studies have found that English-medium teaching increases the workload of instructors (e.g. Maiworm & Wächter 2003: 18; Klaassen 2001), this claim was firmly rejected by all interviewees. They emphasised that compiling new course materials always requires an effort, regardless of the language of instruction. Most of the interviewees indicated that when they teach in German, they might even find themselves struggling to find the correct terminology and expressions. Some indicated that when teaching through English their discourse is not as nuanced, and jokes and anecdotes might occasionally come across a bit clumsily. This finding is in line with those of Wilkinson (2010b) as well as Dafouz and Núñez (2009: 104), who also observed a lack of nuance and a reduction of idiomatic expressions in the teaching of non-native speakers in English-medium lectures. One interviewee identified the fact that he might not be that eloquent in English as a chance to establish rapport with the students, since the 'we are all in the same boat'-notion turned out to be beneficial for the student–teacher relationship (cf. Smit 2010a: 275).

This observation might bear relation to another striking finding regarding teaching styles. The analysis of the course descriptions revealed that the English-taught MA programmes investigated are highly interactive. Instead of teacher-fronted lectures, teaching methods include student presentations, discussion-based case study teaching, peer feedback, Q & A sessions with industry experts, etc. Research into lecturing behaviour in English-medium settings indicates that increased interactivity might even correlate with the use of English as the language of instruction (e.g. Dafouz, Núñez & Sancho 2007; Morell 2004). However, the interviewees pointed out that expert-centred lectures, wherein students are merely listeners, are more frequent at the bachelor's level and not the right format for these specialised MA programmes. They also argued that these interactive teaching styles result from the relatively small student groups and from the fact that methods such as case study teaching are typical for the Anglo-American textbooks they use. Most of the programme directors explicitly stressed that, from their point of view, increased interactivity in their programmes is not directly related to the use of English as the language of instruction. The question of whether there is actually a difference in terms of interactivity between English-medium and L1 lectures again falls outside the scope of the present research project. However, the subjective assessment of content teachers may not directly reflect classroom reality, since a study on the differences between lecturing in a foreign language and in one's mother tongue indicated that "teaching through an L2 may entail differences […] which frequently go unnoticed" (Dafouz Milne & Núñez Perucha 2010: 230).

As already discussed above, the programme directors were confident about the teaching staff's good command of English. The question of whether it was reasonable to test the English proficiency of those teaching in the programmes proved to be a rather delicate one. Most of the interviewees simply found it absurd to ask instructors, who are usually high-ranked experts in their fields, to sit an English test. Whereas the idea appears to be quite inconceivable in the Austrian setting, there are European institutions where it became commonplace to test the English proficiency of the staff teaching in EMPs. For instance, the University of Copenhagen introduced a certification of teachers who lecture in English (Cancino 2011:149–150). Similarly, Delft University of Technology decided to test the language proficiency of the lecturers after students had voiced complaints about the quality of English-medium instruction (Klaassen & Bos 2010:61). The university management in Delft even wants the lecturers to reach a C2 level according to the CEFR in order to be qualified to teach in EMPs (Klaassen & Bos 2010:74–75).

However, not all of the programme directors at WU rejected the idea of using an English proficiency test as a method of quality assurance. For example, it was suggested that problem areas identified in such a test could be the basis for tailor-made training courses. This would then also require the development of a customised testing instrument, because even though IELTS or TOEFL would be convenient to use, "they would not fully reflect the communicative tasks faced by university lecturers, i.e. they would not fully represent the domain of university teaching" (Kling & Staehr 2011:214–215). An example of good practice is provided by the University of Copenhagen which developed and implemented the Test of Oral English Proficiency for Academic Staff (TOEPAS) to assess "whether university lecturers have sufficient oral proficiency for coping with the communicative demands of English-medium instruction" (Kling & Staehr 2011:214). Although the university management implemented the TOEPAS as a quality management tool, it turned out to be a useful starting point for tailor-made teacher training (Kling & Staehr 2011:213).

Currently, there are two teacher training classes with a focus on English-medium instruction offered at WU, i.e. 'Teaching in English' and 'English in the classroom'. Although none of the interviewees had ever attended one of these courses, other forms of training are provided in their programmes. For instance, the teaching staff of *Quantitative Finance* regularly receive training in teaching methods (e.g. case study teaching) which includes feedback by a language teacher. Still, the general attitude towards developing the English proficiency of the content experts teaching in the EMPs remains somewhat reserved as most programme directors believe that the majority of the faculty already has a fluent command of English.

Conclusions

Since the number of English-medium programmes in business studies is expected to rise steadily, more research evidence is needed to understand the potentially far-reaching implications these programmes have at organisational and pedagogical levels. The study presented in this paper aimed at advancing the understanding of this reality by providing a comprehensive overview of the spread of English-medium programmes at business faculties across Austria and by uncovering distinctive features in programme and curriculum design. Ultimately, the findings are expected to contribute to the development of good practice guidelines meant to assist the implementation and operation of EMPs. In order to meet these objectives, data gathering procedures integrated macro and micro perspectives.

Five main findings emerged from the macro data regarding the distribution and characteristics of EMPs across Austrian business faculties. To begin with, WU and the University of Innsbruck are clearly the main providers of EMPs. Together they offer more than half of all English-taught degree courses in business and economics in Austria. Both institutions pride themselves on the relatively high positions they hold in international higher education rankings amongst other prestigious business schools. A further point of interest concerns the implementation years, since 30% of all programmes which currently exist were implemented in 2009/10. This boom most likely bears a causal relation to the official launch of the European Higher Education Area (EHEA) in 2010. It can thus be argued that the peak of the Bologna reforms was accompanied by the introduction of numerous English-taught degree programmes at Austrian business faculties.

In the context of entry requirements, obvious disparities between institutions came to the fore. While 57% of all EMPs require applicants to submit a TOEFL or IELTS score, some programmes accept school-leaving certificates, and for others, standardised English tests are only mandatory for students from outside the European Economic Area. The common assumption that students from EU or EAA states possess the necessary English skills to cope with the demands of English-medium instruction (Räisänen & Fortanet-Gómez 2008b: 43; Wilkinson 2008a: 174) has been challenged by research in recent years (e.g. Hellekjaer 2009, 2010). The second category of entry requirements is supposed to prove the aptitude of prospective students. The GMAT or GRE certificates, the two firmly established tests in this category, are only mandatory for 27% of the EMPs. One could argue that the submission of a GMAT or GRE score ensures comparability between degrees and fairness in the selection process since the applicants' educational backgrounds diverge widely. However, in this context it remains questionable as to whether it is actually worthwhile to strive for a uniform admission policy, since the programmes' specialisations and consequential target groups are so varied. In fact, the Austrian higher education system as such is rather heterogeneous which does not allow for rigid admission policies. Even though the introduction of the 3-cycle degree structure was a move towards more uniformity, admission requirements still have to meet the specifics of the programmes and those of the system at large.

Generally, one has to bear in mind that standardised entrance tests such as the IELTS, TOEFL, GMAT or GRE were originally developed for universities in English-speaking countries and that it is yet to be verified as to whether they are suitable for English-taught degree programmes in non-English speaking environments (Wilkinson 2008a: 174). In fact, when it comes to measuring the English proficiency of applicants, the setting even calls for higher, not lower, requirements (Wilkinson 2008a: 180).

On the micro level, the study also identified several key facts about EMPs at WU. Among the most striking findings are those concerning the curriculum design of EMPs. The results point towards a lack of awareness of the ESP element in English-medium business education, as only 11% of the courses in the programmes investigated can be classified as ESP. Language learning in EMPs is frequently considered incidental (cf. Wilkinson 2010b) and a high level of English proficiency is simply assumed on enrolment. Surprisingly, collaboration with the specialist language teachers and researchers at WU's Department of Foreign Language Business Communication is rare and only one ESP course designed jointly by content and language experts was identified. This tailor-made course should serve as a model in the future, since it actually represents the ideal context for ESP teaching in EMPs in which the language specialists hone students' discipline-specific language skills with tasks and materials closely related to their content classes (cf. Räisänen & Fortanet-Gómez 2008b: 42; Wilkinson 2008b: 55). Despite the lack of focus on ESP, the analysis also showed that about a third of all content classes explicitly state language learning aims in their course descriptions. This challenges the common assumption that language learning objectives are not actively pursued in English-medium teaching at the tertiary level (cf. Järvinen 2008: 78). However, if students do not have the chance to develop their English proficiency in ESP courses, it remains questionable as to whether the stated language learning objectives can be met.

The analysis of the course descriptions also revealed that the teaching formats in the programmes are highly interactive, i.e. expert-centred lectures are scarce. However, the interviewees stressed that these interactive teaching styles are not a result of the use of English as the medium of instruction, but typical for such specialised MA programmes. Furthermore, interviewees were not only confident about their didactic skills but also of their linguistic competences. As regards the teaching staff's English proficiency, they consider it to be at a high level and, in contrast to common practices at other European universities (cf. Cancino 2011:149–150; Klaassen & Bos 2010:61; Kling & Staehr 2011:214–215; Costa and Fortanet-Gómez, both in this volume), they did not think it reasonable to test it. The interviews exposed a socio-cultural particularity about the Austrian context in which the expertise of a renowned university professor stands in direct relation to his or her language competence. In other words, questioning the teachers' language competence would also mean challenging their professional knowledge. This view is further promoted by the lack of explicit policies and the fact that teaching in English is taken for granted rather than rewarded. These observations call on applied linguistics to clarify the role and relevance of the language of instruction in English-medium programmes.

The discussion of selected key findings has exposed some limitations of the study which primarily concern classroom reality. In other words, it lies outside the scope of this project to investigate how discipline-specific language learning is supported in these courses; whether the stated language learning aims are fulfilled; how interactive the teaching in these programmes actually is; and if instructors possess the necessary English skills to teach in these programmes. Nevertheless, this snapshot of the status quo of English-medium degree programmes at Austrian business faculties produced illuminating insights which could also be valid in other contexts. Despite its local character, the findings of this study could promote the development of institutional policies and assist programme designers in the implementation, operation and development of EMPs.

Notes

1. The tertiary education sector in Austria comprises a variety of higher education institutions, including state and private universities, colleges, academies and universities of applied sciences (Eurydice 2010b:5). In order to ensure comparability, the scope of the status quo survey was restricted to the nine state universities, seven of which offer programmes which are entirely taught through English: Alpen Adria University of Klagenfurt, Graz University of Technology, Johannes Kepler University Linz, University of Innsbruck, University of Vienna, Vienna University of Economics and Business (WU), Vienna University of Technology.

2. In the academic year 2011/12 the total number of EMPs at WU was 7, i.e. 4 MA and 3 PhD programmes (cf. Figure 1). Since there is one programme director in charge of all PhD programmes at WU, 5 interviews were conducted, while in two cases 2 interviewees were present.

3. The three-year, EU-funded, pan-European LANQUA project aimed at mapping "the field of languages within higher education" and identified "key quality assurance and enhancement strategies for practitioners" (The Language Network for Quality Assurance (LANQUA) 2010).

4. The Graduate Management Admission Test (GMAT) evaluates verbal, mathematical, analytical and writing skills. The exam is meant to assess applicants' qualifications for business and management degree programmes (Graduate Management Admission Council).

5. The GRE exam measures applicants' problem-solving abilities, quantitative reasoning as well as their critical thinking and analytical skills. The GRE test is not restricted to business studies per se, and thus scores can also be used to apply for degree programmes in other disciplines (Educational Testing Service (ETS) 2012).

References

Airey, J. 2009. Science, language and literacy. Case studies of learning in Swedish university physics. *Uppsala Dissertations from the Faculty of Science and Technology 81*. Uppsala: Uppsala Universitet.

Airey, J. 2011. The disciplinary literacy discussion matrix: a heuristic tool for initiating collaboration in higher education. *Across the Disciplines* 8(3), ⟨http://wac.colostate.edu/atd/clil/airey.cfm⟩ (10 April 2012).

Benelux Bologna Secretariat. 2007–2010. The official Bologna process website July 2007–June 2010, ⟨http:// www.ond.vlaanderen.be/hogeronderwijs/bologna/⟩ (11 January 2011).

Cancino, R. 2011. Language policy, language planning and language teaching at Danish universities. In *Policies, Principles, Practices: New Directions in Foreign Language Education in the Era of Educational Globalization*, R. Cancino, L. Dam, & K. Jæger (eds), 138–160. Newcastle upon Tyne, UK: Cambridge Scholars Publishers.

Confederation of EU Rectors' Conference and the Association of European Universities (CRE). 2000. *The Bologna Declaration on the European Space for Higher Education: An Explanation*, ⟨http://ec.europa.eu/ education/policies/educ/bologna/bologna.pdf⟩ (10 April 2012).

Dafouz, E. & Núñez, B. 2009. CLIL in tertiary education: devising a new learning landscape. In *CLIL Across Educational Levels: Experiences from Primary, Secondary and Tertiary Contexts*, E. Dafouz & M. Guerrini (eds.), 101–112. London: Richmond.

Dafouz, E. & Núñez a, B. 2010. Metadiscursive devices in university lectures: A contrastive analysis of L1 and L2 teacher performance. In *Language Use and Language Learning in CLIL Classrooms*, C. Dalton-Puffer, T. Nikula & U. Smit (eds), 213–231. Amsterdam: John Benjamins.

Dafouz, E., Núñez, B. & Sancho, C. 2007. Analysing stance in a CLIL university context: non-native speaker use of personal pronouns and modal verbs. *The International Journal of Bilingual Education and Bilingualism* 10(5): 647–662.

Educational Testing Service (ETS). 2012. *About the GRE*®, ⟨http://www.ets.org/gre/revised_general/about⟩ (10 April 2012).

European Ministers of Education. 1999. *The Bologna Declaration of 19 June 1999: Joint Declaration of the European Ministers of Education*, ⟨http://www.ond.vlaanderen.be/hogeronderwijs/bologna/documents/ MDC/BOLOGNA_DECLARATION1.pdf⟩ (10 April 2012).

European Ministers of Higher Education. 2010. *Budapest-Vienna Declaration on the European Higher Education Area*, ⟨http://www.ond.vlaanderen.be/hogeronderwijs/bologna/2010_conference/documents/Budapest-Vienna_Declaration.pdf⟩ (10 April 2012).

Eurydice. 2010a. *Structures of Education and Training Systems in Europe: Austria 2009/10 Edition*, ⟨http:// eacea.ec.europa.eu/education/eurydice/documents/eurybase/structures/041_AT_EN.pdf⟩ (10 April 2012).

Eurydice. 2010b. *The Structure of the European Education Systems 2010/11: Schematic Diagrams*, ⟨http://eacea.ec.europa.eu/education/eurydice/documents/tools/108EN.pdf⟩ (10 April 2012).

Financial Times European Business School Ranking. ⟨http://rankings.ft.com/businessschoolrankings/european-business-school-rankings-2011⟩ (10 February 2012).

Graduate Management Admission Council. *The GMAT*®: Test Structure &Overview, ⟨http://www.mba.com/ the-gmat/test-structure-and-overview.aspx⟩ (10 April 2012).

Greere, A. & Räsänen, A. 2008. *Year One Report: LANQUA Subproject on Content and Language Integrated Learning — Redefining 'CLIL' towards Multilingual Competence*, ⟨http://www.archive.lanqua.eu/files/ Year1Report_CLIL_ForUpload_WithoutAppendices_0.pdf⟩ (10 April 2012).

Hellekjaer, G.O. 2007. The implementation of undergraduate level English-medium programs in Norway: an explorative case study. In *Researching Content and Language Integration in Higher Education*, R. Wilkinson & V. Zegers (eds), 68–81. Nijmegen: Valkhof Pers.

Hellekjaer, G.O. 2009. Academic English reading proficiency at the university level: A Norwegian case study. *Reading in a Foreign Language* 21(2): 198–222.

Hellekjaer, G.O. 2010. Language matters: assessing lecture comprehension in Norwegian English-medium higher education. In *Language Use and Language Learning in CLIL Classrooms*, C. Dalton-Puffer, T. Nikula, & U. Smit, 233–258. Amsterdam: John Benjamins.

Horak, A. 2010. *Der gemeinsame europäische Referenzrahmen für Sprachen in der Unterrichtspraxis: Bildungsstandards — für höchste Qualität an Österreichs Schulen*. Graz: ÖSZ Österreichisches Sprachen-Kompetenz-Zentrum, ⟨http://www.oesz.at/download/publikationen/Broschuere_interaktiv.pdf⟩ (10 April 2012).

Järvinen, H.-M. 2008. Learning contextualized language: implications for tertiary foreign-language-medium education. In *Foreign-Language-Medium Instruction in Tertiary Education: A Tool for Enhancing Language Learning*, E. Rauto & L. Saarikoski, 77–85. Vaasan Ammattikorkeakoulu: Vaasan Ammattikorkeakoulu, University of Applied Sciences Publications.

Klaassen, R.G. 2001. The international university curriculum: Challenges in English-medium engineering education. Unpublished PhD thesis. Delft University of Technology.

Klaassen, R.G. 2008. Preparing lecturers for English-medium instruction. In *Realizing Content and Language Integration in Higher Education*, R. Wilkinson & V. Zegers (eds), 32–42. Maastricht: Maastricht University.

Klaassen, R.G. & Bos, M. 2010. English language screening for scientific staff at Delft University of Technology. *Hermes — Journal of Language and Communication Studies* 45: 61–75.

Kling, J. & Staehr, L.S. 2011. Assessment and assistance: developing university lecturers' skills through certification feedback. In *Policies, Principles, Practices: New Directions in Foreign Language Education in the Era of Educational Globalization*, R. Cancino, L. Dam, & K. Jæger (eds), 213–245. Newcastle upon Tyne, UK: Cambridge Scholars Publishers.

Knight, J. 2008. *Higher Education in Turmoil: The Changing World of Internationalisation*. Rotterdam: Sense Publishers.

Lehtonen, T., Pitkänen, K., Siddall, R. & Virkkunen-Fullenwider, A. 2009. A quick-and-dirty SWOT analysis on Master's degree programmes conducted in English in non-English environments. In *Bi- and Multilingual Universities: European Perspectives and Beyond: Conference Proceedings Bolzano-Bozen, 20–22 September 2007*. D. Veronesi & C. Nickenig, 265–273. Bozen: Bozen Bolzana University Press.

Leiden Ranking. ⟨http://www.leidenranking.com/⟩ (10 February 2012).

Maiworm, F. & Wächter, B. 2002. *English-Language-Taught Degree Programmes in European Higher Education: Trends and Success Factors*. Bonn: Lemmens.

Maiworm, F. & Wächter, B. 2003. *Englischsprachige Studiengänge in Europa: Merkmale, Impulse, Erfolgsfaktoren*, ⟨http://www.stifterverband.info/publikationen_und_podcasts/positionen_dokumentationen/englischsprachige_studiengaenge_in_europa_2003.pdf⟩ (10 April 2012).

Morell, T. 2004. Interactive lecture discourse for university EFL students. *English for Specific Purposes* 23: 325–238.

Räisänen, C.A. & Fortanet-Gómez, I. 2008a. Introduction: English for specific purposes after the Bologna reform. In *ESP in European Higher Education: Integrating Language and Content*, I. Fortanet-Gómez & C.A. Räisänen (eds), 1–7. Amsterdam: John Benjamins.

Räisänen, C.A. & Fortanet-Gómez, I. 2008b. The state of ESP teaching and learning in western European higher education after Bologna. In *ESP in European Higher Education: Integrating Language and Content*, I. Fortanet-Gómez & C.A. Räisänen (eds), 11–51. Amsterdam: John Benjamins.

Smit, U. 2003. English as lingua franca (ELF) as medium of learning in a hotel management educational program: an applied linguistic approach. *VIEWS — Vienna English Working Papers* 12(2): 40–74, ⟨http://anglistik.univie.ac.at/views/archive/⟩ (6 March 2012).

Smit, U. 2010a. CLIL in an English as a lingua franca (ELF) classroom: On explaining terms and expressions interactively. In *Language Use and Language Learning in CLIL Classrooms*. C. Dalton-Puffer, T. Nikula & U. Smit (eds), 259–277. Amsterdam: John Benjamins.

Smit, U. 2010b. *English as a Lingua Franca in Higher Education: A Longitudinal Study of Classroom Discourse*. Berlin: De Gruyter.

The Language Network for Quality Assurance (LANQUA). 2010. *A quality toolkit for languages: Frame of reference for quality in languages in higher education*, ⟨http://www.lanqua.eu/sites/default/files/LanQua_quality_model.pdf⟩ (8 February 2012).

Times Higher Education World University Ranking. ⟨http://www.timeshighereducation.co.uk/world-university-rankings/⟩ (10 February 2012)

University of Innsbruck. 2011. *Rankings: International Standing*, ⟨http://www.uibk.ac.at/universitaet/profil/rankings.html⟩ (5 February 2012).

Unterberger, B. & Wilhelmer, N. 2011. English-medium education in economics and business studies: Capturing the status quo at Austrian universities. *ITL – International Journal of Applied Linguistics* 161: 90–110.

Vienna University of Economics and Business. 2011. *Accreditations & Rankings*, ⟨http://www.wu.ac.at/strategy/en/accreditations/international/ft⟩ (5 February 2012).

Wächter, B. 2003. Englischsprachige Studiengänge in Europa. *die hochschule* 1: 88–108.

Wächter, B. & Maiworm, F. 2008. *English-Taught Programmes in European Higher Education: The Picture in 2007*. Bonn: Lemmens Medien.

Wilkinson, R. 2005a. The impact of language on teaching content: views from the content teacher. Paper presented at the *Conference on Bi- and Multilingual Universities: Challenges and Future Prospects*, Helsinki.

Wilkinson, R. 2005b. Where is English taking universities? *Guardian Weekly*, March 18, ⟨http://www.guardian.co.uk/theguardian/2005/mar/17/guardianweekly.guardianweekly1#history-link-box⟩ (16 August 2010).

Wilkinson, R. 2008a. English-taught study courses: principles and practice. In *English in Academia. Catalyst or Carrier?*, C. Gnutzmann (ed), 169–182. Tübingen: Gunter Narr.

Wilkinson, R. 2008b. Locating the ESP space in problem-based learning: English-medium degree programmes from a post-Bologna perspective. In *ESP in European Higher Education: Integrating Language and Content*, I. Fortanet-Gómez & C.A. Räisänen (eds), 55–73. Amsterdam: Benjamins.

Wilkinson, R. 2010a. English-medium instruction at a Dutch university: What have we learned from a quarter of a century experience? Paper presented at *The Norwegian Forum for English for Academic Purposes (NFEAP)*, Oslo.

Wilkinson, R. 2010b. What if all business education were in English, would we notice the difference? Paper presented at Languages in Business Education, Brussels.

WU — Vienna University of Economics and Business. 2011. *Facts & Figures About WU*, ⟨http://www.wu.ac.at/press/about/structure/about/publications/publ_pdfs/factsfigures.pdf⟩ (10 April 2012).

Author's affiliation and e-mail address

Vienna University of Economics and Business (WU), Austria

barbara.unterberger@wu.ac.at

A postscript on institutional motivations, research concerns and professional implications

Christiane Dalton-Puffer

From the point of view of AILA's research network *CLIL and Immersion Education: Applied Linguistic Perspectives* this volume finally does justice to a strand of interest that has been part of the network from its inception. As the editors rightly point out in the introduction, ReN events and publications during the network's first period have focused more strongly on school-level education than on the post-secondary sector, and so it is truly timely that this volume of *AILA Review* should redress the balance.

While the academic world has always been international, the dimensions of this internationalisation have assumed truly global proportions during the last two decades, affecting not only research circles but higher education in general. So why, one might ask, put a geographical focus on Europe? The case is argued convincingly by the editors by referring to the situation at hand. European countries feature historically deeply entrenched and well-developed higher education systems that have evolved in the respective national languages since the middle of the 19th century; this seemingly stable situation is being unsettled by the exponential growth of English-medium teaching in many institutions and subject areas. Wächter observes that such "a fast growth-rate" points towards the fact that we are witnessing "an early-stage phenomenon" (Wächter 2008: 4). In other words the research presented in this volume opens windows on a highly dynamic situation which has not only raised heated debates (e.g. Carli & Ammon 2007; Phillipson 2009; Zegers & Wilkinson 2005) but also confronts the people involved with considerable challenges on a day-to-day basis as "internationalism is omnipresent and intertwined with local pursuits in complex ways" (Mauranen 2010: 7).

In combination, the contributions in this collection weave a multifaceted picture of the European experience with regard to the ongoing surge in English-medium university teaching, ranging from individual courses to entire curricula being administered in that language. As one reviews the motives and aims which institutions and stakeholders appear to connect with the introduction of English-medium teaching one can, I wish to argue, discern three broad types of motivation: Strategic, Pedagogical and Substantial.

1. Strategic motives:
    Universities aim to attract high-capability students and to promote internationalisation so as to attract international students and staff. A further motive is the bid for membership among a group of 'elite' institutions.
2. Pedagogical motives:
    Preparing students for an international job-market and/or international academic life as well as offering them opportunities for widening their lingua-cultural horizons is another reason for introducing EMI.

AILA Review 25 (2012), 101–103. DOI 10.1075/aila.25.07dal
ISSN 1461–0213 / E-ISSN 1570–5595 © John Benjamins Publishing Company

3.   Substantial motives:

In many areas today the latest content and ongoing research in the field is communicated exclusively via English in the scientific community; there may be very little L1 literature (or even none) in the specialised and/or advanced areas of the field.

The contributions to this volume furnish examples for all of these motives even though they may not be considered equally important by the participants in each context.

Despite the special dynamism present in European higher education today, I would not like to ignore the concerns shared across the AILA Research Network as a whole. The fact that researchers with different contextual orientations have been interacting and cooperating profitably and successfully since 2006 is witness enough that there is a significant number of common concerns where a shared discourse helps to clarify the issues and to sharpen theoretical and methodological notions. Without making a claim for being exhaustive I would like to mention the following:

a.   the fact that it is nearly always English which is meant by 'language', be it in CLIL or ICLHE: English as a lingua franca is an issue in both cases but higher education has progressed somewhat further with regard to considering the implications;

b.   the fact that labels like CLIL, EMI or ICLHE actually cover a wide range of implementation types from fully English-medium programmes to curricula with a small number of English-medium subjects; and the related fact that educational decision makers are not always clear about the exact aims pursued by which type of implementation;

c.   the previous situation arises because CLIL, EMI and ICLHE are frequently treated as if they were terminological (i.e. having a clear cut definition), or more problematic still, as some kind of theory of language learning or language use rather than what they are, namely convenient shorthand or brands, which stand for bundles of highly contextualized actual measures and are frequently charged with implicit value judgements.

In reaction to this last point in particular, the core motivation of all members of the ReN has been to counterbalance the prevalence of declarations and claims with theoretically explicit empirical research that takes into account the high degree of contextualisation of specific implementations while examining the actual language use in CLIL and ICLHE classrooms as well as the perceptions and beliefs of participants. As readers will have noticed, both these research orientations are also represented in the present volume.

Subject-matter teaching in English raises highly relevant questions regarding the role of English as an educational lingua franca, a subject which the contributions in this volume also begin to explore (see also Smit 2010) and which, no doubt, we will see a continued discussion of. But the practices described in the studies are intriguing to applied linguists not only in terms of their theoretical and empirical research interests. They also affect them on a very direct professional level: subject-matter teaching in English transgresses well-established disciplinary and system-inherent borders creating considerable insecurities along the way. The language teaching profession and especially ESP lecturers at universities are justifiedly on the alert. After all, a widespread implementation of English-medium teaching that understands itself purely as an instance of 'ELF use' and leaves language learning either completely out of the picture or hands it over to implicit mechanisms while the focus is on disciplinary content is likely to have profound consequences on the profession in very real terms of jobs and income. In this respect the research conducted on ICLHE is also an exercise in professional self-reflection and intervention in the interest of a wholesome development of the profession.

References

Carli, A. & Ammon, U. (eds.) 2007. *Linguistic Inequality in Scientific Communication Today. AILA Review*, 20.

Mauranen, A. 2010. Features of English as a lingua franca in academia. *Helsinki English Studies* 6: 6–28.

Phillipson, R. 2009. English in higher education: Panacea or pandemic? In *English in Denmark: Language Policy, Internationalisation and University Teaching*, P. Harder (ed.), 29–57. Special issue of *ANGLES on the English-Speaking World* 9.

Smit, U. 2010. *English as a Lingua Franca in Higher Education. A Longitudinal Study of Classroom Discourse.* Berlin: De Gruyter.

Wächter, B. 2008. Teaching in English on the rise in European education. *International Higher Education* 52: 3–4.

Zegers, V. & Wilkinson, R. 2005. Squaring the pyramid: Internationalisation, plurilingualism, and the university, ⟨http://www.palmenia.helsinki.fi/congress/bilingual2005/presentations/zegers.pdf⟩ (13 August 2012).

Author's affiliation and e-mail address

Universität Wien, Austria

christiane.dalton-puffer@univie.ac.at

New Dictionaries

Words are never used in isolation but in combination, and not with any word but only with certain specific words.
To use a language properly the appropriate combinations must be used.
So every language has its own preferences in word combinations, misleading a non-native learner into making mistakes influenced by his own language.

Dizionario Combinatorio Compatto Italiano

A cura di Vincenzo Lo Cascio

ItalNed Foundation / University of Amsterdam

This dictionary reconstructs the frame to which 3,000 Italian entries belong and aims to help non-Italian speakers with an advanced linguistic competence to find the appropriate word combinations for communicating in Italian. Moreover, this dictionary can also be useful for native speakers who want to improve their lexical choices in writing and speaking Italian.

The dictionary, contrary to ordinary monolingual and bilingual dictionaries, systematically lists word combinations (almost 90,000), explaining and/or exemplifying them.

2012. xxvi, 642 pp.

PB   978 90 272 1193 4 EUR 39.00 / USD 59.00
E-BOOK 978 90 272 7465 6 EUR 39.00 / USD 59.00

Dizionario Combinatorio Italiano

A cura di Vincenzo Lo Cascio

ItalNed Foundation / University of Amsterdam

This dictionary reconstructs the frame to which 6,500 Italian entries belong and aims to help non-Italian speakers with an advanced linguistic competence to find the appropriate word combinations for communicating in Italian. Moreover, this dictionary can also be useful for native speakers who want to improve their lexical choices in writing and speaking Italian, as for translators, business people, researchers, teachers, and students.

The dictionary, contrary to ordinary monolingual and bilingual dictionaries, systematically lists (nearly 220,000) word combinations, with explanations and with examples (approx. 12,000) to demonstrate their usage.

2013. xxii, 1387 pp. (2 vols. set)

HB   978 90 272 1202 3 EUR 195.00 / USD 293.00
E-BOOK 978 90 272 7231 7 EUR 195.00 / USD 293.00

For more information see *www.benjamins.com*

Task-Based Language Teaching in Foreign Language Contexts

Research and implementation

Edited by Ali Shehadeh and Christine A. Coombe

UAE University / Dubai Men's College

This volume extends the Task-Based Language Teaching: Issues, Research and Practice books series by deliberately exploring the potential of task-based language teaching (TBLT) in a range of EFL contexts. It is specifically devoted to providing empirical accounts about how TBLT practice is being developed and researched in diverse educational contexts, particularly where English is not the dominant language. By including contributions from settings as varied as Japan, China, Korea, Venezuela, Turkey, Spain, and France, this collection of 13 studies provides strong indications that the research and implementation of TBLT in EFL settings is both on the rise and interestingly diverse, not least because it must respond to the distinct contexts, constraints, and possibilities of foreign language learning. The book will be of interest to SLA researchers and students in applied linguistics and TESOL. It will also be of value to course designers and language teachers who come from a broad range of formal and informal educational settings encompassing a wide range of ages and types of language learners.

[Task-Based Language Teaching, 4] 2012. xix, 364 pp.

HB	978 90 272 0723 4 EUR 99.00	/ USD 149.00
PB	978 90 272 0724 1 EUR 33.00	/ USD 49.95
E-BOOK 978 90 272 7342 0 EUR 99.00	/ USD 149.00	

Task-Based Language Teaching from the Teachers' Perspective

Insights from New Zealand

Martin East

The University of Auckland

Task-based language teaching (TBLT) is being encouraged as part of a major overhaul of the entire school languages curriculum in New Zealand. However, teachers often struggle with understanding what TBLT is, and how to make TBLT work in classrooms. Using the stories that emerged from a series of interviews with teachers (the curriculum implementers) and with advisors (the curriculum leaders), this book highlights the possibilities for TBLT innovation in schools. It also identifies the constraints, and proposes how these might be addressed. The result is a book that, whilst rooted in a particular local context, provides a valuable sourcebook of teacher stories that have relevance for a wide range of people working in a diverse range of contexts. This book will be of genuine interest to all those who wish to understand more about TBLT innovation, and the opportunities and challenges it brings.

[Task-Based Language Teaching, 3] 2012. xix, 259 pp.

HB	978 90 272 0721 0 EUR 99.00	/ USD 149.00
PB	978 90 272 0722 7 EUR 33.00	/ USD 49.95
E-BOOK 978 90 272 8182 1 EUR 99.00	/ USD 149.00	

For more information see *www.benjamins.com*

Second Language Interaction in Diverse Educational Contexts

Edited by Kim McDonough and Alison Mackey

Concordia University / Georgetown University

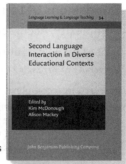

This volume brings together empirical research that explores interaction in a wide range of educational settings. It includes work that takes a cognitive, brain-based approach to studying interaction, as well as studies that take a social, contextual perspective. Interaction is defined quite broadly, with many chapters focusing on oral interaction as is typical in the field, while other chapters report work that involves interaction between learners and technology. Several studies describe the linguistic and discourse features of interaction between learners and their interlocutors, but others demonstrate how interaction can serve other purposes, such as to inform placement decisions. The chapters in the book collectively illustrate the diversity of contemporary approaches to interaction research, investigating interactions with different interlocutors (learner-learner, learner-teacher), in a variety of environments (classrooms, interactive testing environments, conversation groups) and through different modalities (oral and written, face-to-face and technology-mediated).

[Language Learning & Language Teaching, 34] 2013. xiv, 315 pp. + index

HB   978 90 272 1309 9 EUR 99.00 / USD 149.00
PB   978 90 272 1310 5 EUR 36.00 / USD   54.00
E-BOOK   978 90 272 7234 8 EUR 99.00 / USD 149.00

Linguistics for Intercultural Education

Edited by Fred Dervin and Anthony J. Liddicoat

University of Helsinki / University of South Australia

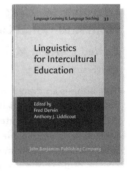

The issue of intercultural learning has been tackled, amongst others, in the fields of education, language education and applied linguistics. In spite of the extensive literature on the subject, there is still much which needs to be done to address the ways in which linguistics itself can contribute to intercultural education. The 8 chapters by internationally-renowned scholars highlight different ways of using it both in the classroom and in researching intercultural education. The following approaches are covered: Critical Discourse Analysis, Énonciation, Conversation Analysis and Pragmatics. The introduction to the volume also offers a useful and comprehensive survey of the debates around the polysemic notion of the 'intercultural'. The book will appeal to an international readership of students, scholars and professionals across a wide range of disciplines, interested in making intercultural education more effective.

[Language Learning & Language Teaching, 33] 2013. vi, 196 pp. + index

HB   978 90 272 1307 5 EUR 95.00 / USD 143.00
PB   978 90 272 1308 2 EUR 33.00 / USD   49.95
E-BOOK   978 90 272 7235 5 EUR 95.00 / USD 143.00

For more information see *www.benjamins.com*

Dimensions of L2 Performance and Proficiency
Complexity, Accuracy and Fluency in SLA

Edited by Alex Housen, Folkert Kuiken and Ineke Vedder
University of Brussels / University of Amsterdam

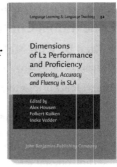

Research into complexity, accuracy and fluency (CAF) as basic dimensions of second language performance, proficiency and development has received increased attention in SLA. However, the larger picture in this field of research is often obscured by the breadth of scope, multiple objectives and lack of clarity as to how complexity, accuracy and fluency should be defined, operationalized and measured. The present volume showcases current research on CAF by bringing together eleven contributions from renowned international researchers in the field. These contributions not only add to the body of empirical knowledge about L2 use and L2 development by bringing new research findings to light but they also address fundamental theoretical and methodological issues by responding to questions about the nature, manifestation, development and assessment of CAF as multifaceted constructs. Collectively, the chapters in this book illustrate the converging and sometimes diverging approaches that different disciplines bring to CAF research.

[Language Learning & Language Teaching, 32] 2012. xii, 305 pp.

HB	978 90 272 1305 1	EUR 99.00 / USD 149.00
PB	978 90 272 1306 8	EUR 36.00 / USD 54.00
E-BOOK	978 90 272 7326 0	EUR 99.00 / USD 149.00

Learning-to-Write and Writing-to-Learn in an Additional Language

Edited by Rosa M. Manchón
University of Murcia

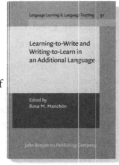

This book is a pioneer attempt to bridge the gap between the fields of second language acquisition (SLA) and second and foreign language (L2) writing. Its ultimate aim is to advance our understanding of written language learning by compiling a collection of theoretical meta-reflections and empirical studies that shed new light on two crucial dimensions of the theory and research in the field: first, the manner in which L2 users learn to express themselves in writing (the learning-to-write dimension), and, second, the manner in which the engagement in written output practice can contribute to developing competences in an L2 (the writing-to-learn dimension). These two areas of disciplinary inquiry have up until now developed separately: the learning-to-write dimension has been the cornerstone of L2 writing research, whereas the writing-to-learn one has been theorized and researched within SLA studies, hence the relevance of the book for exploring L2 writing-SLA interfaces.

[Language Learning & Language Teaching, 31] 2011. xii, 263 pp.

HB	978 90 272 1303 7	EUR 99.00 / USD 149.00
PB	978 90 272 1304 4	EUR 36.00 / USD 54.00
E-BOOK	978 90 272 8483 9	EUR 99.00 / USD 149.00

For more information see *www.benjamins.com*